This is my faith journey.

Nihil obstat:
   Msgr. Michael Heintz,
   Censor librorum

Imprimatur:
   ✠Most Rev. Kevin C. Rhoades,
   Bishop of Fort Wayne–South Bend
   September 20, 2019

PRINTED IN THE UNITED STATES OF AMERICA.

Cover, interior design, and composition by Laurie Nelson, Agápe Design Studios.

Graphic elements: © iStockphoto.com, © Adobe Stock

Acknowledgments

Allison Gingras wrote the opening and closing prayers for each chapter.

ISBN 978-1-68192-533-2 (Inventory No. T2422)
1. RELIGION—Christian Life—Spiritual growth.
2. RELIGION—Christian Life—Women's Issues.
3. RELIGION—Christianity—Catholic.

LCCN: 2020934670

OUR SUNDAY VISITOR
HUNTINGTON, INDIANA
WWW.OSV.COM

Journals for Catholic Women

Make Every Day Blessed

Living the Liturgical Year

Jennifer Frost

Dedication:

This book is dedicated to my parents, grandparents, and godparents, who gave me the gift of faith; and to my husband and son, who celebrate it with me every day.

Jen Frost

Table of Contents

Introduction

Like many people, I'd be lost without my planner. Inside are all the key events going on in my family's life, as well as upcoming holidays, birthdays, and anniversaries. My planner starts on January 1, New Year's Day, and it marks all the important dates of the year—St. Patrick's Day, the summer solstice, the Fourth of July, Labor Day, Thanksgiving, and so on. The pages of each month are adorned with the prettiest flowers, color coordinated with the appropriate season.

The Catholic Church also has a way of marking time that bears many similarities to my planner: the liturgical year, which is "the temporal structure within which the Church celebrates the holy mysteries of Christ."[1] As a Catholic community, we celebrate our own new year—complete with memorable "New Year's Day" candles—on the first day of Advent. And just as my planner designates birthdays, anniversaries, and the changing seasons, the Church has designated feast days, holy days, and special seasons throughout the year.

If my planner is designed to help me keep track of the day-to-day details of my life, the Church's liturgical calendar is designed to help us remember that all time is also sacred time. The liturgical calendar enables us to make our faith the central point around which everything else flows.

"To live liturgically," says Dr. Chene Heady, author of *Numbering My Days: How the Liturgical Calendar Rearranged My Life*, "is to be aware of the divine meaning and significance of every moment."[2] For example, if we are aware that next Sunday is the Feast of Christ the King, we become open to thinking of Jesus as our leader, pondering our place as one of his disciples and learning more about what it takes to be a good servant. If we are oblivious to these special feasts and celebrations, then next Sunday becomes just another day for tackling our to-do lists or, maybe, cramming in Mass before work and school resume on Monday.

If, however, we live liturgically—that is, if we live intentionally with the changing seasons of Christ's Church—we weave a deeper meaning

and purpose into our everyday lives. We begin each day with a different sort of intentionality, one that goes beyond the to-do list. We see our lives through the eyes of the saints, extend the gift we receive each week at Mass, and go out to make disciples of all the world as God asks us to do.

By living liturgically, we experience the full "mystery of Christ from his Incarnation and Nativity through his Ascension, to Pentecost and the expectation of the blessed hope of the coming of the Lord" (*Catechism*, 1194). Living in such a way has given me the ability to bring elements from the Church's celebrations and traditions into our home, creating a much-needed bridge between our Sunday worship and family life. It is also through our shared traditions that we find and grow in community. Amid the rise of secular "holidays" like Fruitcake Toss Day, Chocolate Cake Day, and Backwards Day, we remember that we already have rich and wonderful celebrations rooted in faith (and fun!). We are created to live together, to grow in unity, and to share in experiences throughout the liturgical year, generation after generation. I invite you to experience the beauty of the liturgical calendar!

1: The Liturgical Year

MAKE EVERY DAY BLESSED

Opening Prayer

Heavenly Father, how remarkable and numerous are the ways you provide throughout the year for my family and me to celebrate together. The Church is blessed with a rhythm of waiting and receiving, hoping and experiencing, fasting and feasting. You generously pour out your love on us throughout the liturgical year.

Open my heart to enter these seven weeks ready to embrace old traditions while discovering new celebrations. Prepare my heart to grow closer to you as I encounter all the glorious and faith-filled ways that I might live my Catholic faith. Infuse my heart with an abundance of your joy, love, and hope so that I may welcome you into my home and all of our celebrations in a more profound way.

Father, I open this chapter with eager anticipation of the lessons and inspirations it contains. There is much about the celebrations and traditions of the Catholic Church that I do not know. In seeking this knowledge of the Church's feasts and observances, I am also seeking a closer relationship with you. Your Word tells me that whenever I seek you, however I seek you, you will

be found. My mind wonders with delight at how much of you I will discover within these pages.

Thank you for your unfailing love and the endless opportunities you give me to grow in my faith. Thank you for your unfathomable love that is always calling me into deeper relationship with you. As I draw closer to you, St. James teaches, you will draw ever closer to me. May every page bring me one step nearer to you. Amen.

On My Heart

Celebrating the Liturgical Calendar

Have you ever heard friends, family, or a fellow parishioner mention the idea of "living liturgically" and wondered what it meant?

I remember fondly the time I first heard that term used by a friend to describe the way we celebrated the many facets of our Catholic faith. We were at a park with our Moms & Kids Ministry, and we were sharing about how we felt both a letdown and a returning sense of calm now that Easter had ended.

I had mixed feelings: I was happy that the busyness of Lent and Easter were behind us, but I missed the opportunities for community and growth that we found in the fish fry dinners, soup suppers, Stations of the Cross, and traditional family celebrations. Each of these activities anchored us as we celebrated the season of Lent, one of the seasons identified in the liturgical calendar.

These "anchors," with their deliberate and intentional observances, provide a way for us to focus our hearts and minds on Christ. Adam was banished from the garden and sent to toil "by the sweat of [his] brow" (Genesis 3:19). There are days when I feel freshly banished from paradise. With piles of laundry to wash and fold, stacks of mail to respond to, meals to prepare, emails to answer, voicemails to return, bills to pay, and little people to care for, preparing an Easter brunch can feel like one more item on the to-do list.

When I think back to my childhood, it's the very traditions of the liturgical year that I hold closest to my heart. These traditions are one of the ways that my great-grandparents passed their values and faith to my grandparents, my grandparents to my parents, and my parents to me. Continuing these traditions, celebrations, and expressions of faith are ways that I, too, can pass along the faith to my family. It's a gift that helps us not only grow closer to Christ but also establish roots and connections within our family and the broader community.

As a mother, it is hard for me not to imagine Joseph and Mary teaching faith traditions to Jesus when he was a child. After all, one of the stories shared in Scripture about Jesus is of his family's pilgrimage to Jerusalem for Passover. Jesus was born to a Jewish family and followed the customs of that faith, including being circumcised according to Jewish law (Luke 2:21). Scripture also reveals that Jesus frequently visited the synagogue (Mark 3), celebrated Passover (John 2:13, 6:4, and 11:55), and observed Old Testament laws (Luke 5:14).

Just as for Mary and Joseph, it's important that we share and pass our Catholic traditions down to our children. It's a way to keep the truth alive, vibrant, and relevant in our daily lives. Catholicism is rich in popular customs and rituals, all created to strengthen our faith and lead us closer to Our Father. Do your family's celebrations of the liturgical year bring you closer to Christ?

The *Catechism of the Catholic Church* is a wonderful resource for learning more about the traditions and teachings of the Catholic faith. The *Catechism* speaks to how—and why—we celebrate feasts and holy days throughout the year: "In the course of the year, moreover, she unfolds the whole mystery of Christ. ... Thus recalling the mysteries of the redemption, she opens up to the faithful the riches of her Lord's powers and merits, so that these are in some way made present in every age; the faithful lay hold of them and are filled with saving grace" (*Catechism*, 1163). In other words, honoring key dates and events in the history of the Church helps us to live more fully in Christ.

Over the centuries, various cultures have developed their own traditions and ways of celebrating the times and seasons of the Church year. Many of those old traditions are being revived and reclaimed by Catholics today. The Church honors and respects these practices of "popular piety" while ensuring that they don't supplant or distort their liturgical and theological sources. The Church's Congregation for Divine Worship issued its *Directory on Popular Piety and the Liturgy* in 2001 to serve that purpose; you'll find it referenced occasionally throughout this book.

Wash, Rinse, Repeat

Can I share something with you? The first time I heard the term "the liturgical cycle," I thought of laundry and the many wash cycles I had waiting for me at home. Although I'd heard the term "liturgical year" before, thinking of it as a cycle—something that is continuously in a state of fluid motion with celebrations at each stage—was a completely different perspective.

When it comes to celebrating the liturgical cycle, it helps to think of the year as a wheel. The Church year begins at the start of Advent and then progresses through Christmas, the first season of Ordinary Time, Lent, Triduum, Easter, and, finally, a second season of Ordinary Time to complete the year. Just as you can celebrate January 1 as the start of the new year, so, too, can you celebrate the first day of Advent as the start of the Church's new year.

Some of the Church's feasts, such as Christmas and St. Patrick's Day, are *fixed*—meaning they're celebrated on the same day year after year. Other dates, like the first Sundays in Advent, Easter, and Pentecost, change each year (more on that later). Remembering which celebrations are fixed and which are *movable*, meaning that they fall on different dates each year, took some time for me to figure out. Suddenly that laundry cycle seemed so much easier to manage!

Just as each of the natural seasons has its own colors, the changing of the liturgical seasons is often heralded by a change in the colors of the liturgical vestments at church. Sewing and fabrics are a passion of mine, and seeing the green banners for Ordinary Time, the purple and rose vestments for Advent and Lent, and the bright whites for Easter Sunday warms my heart.

In celebration of the changing liturgical seasons, we'll occasionally dress liturgically as a family too. When he was younger, my son used to love wearing clothes that matched our priest's vestments: "Mommy, look! I have on green, and Fr. Mike has on green! We're the same!" Now, mind you, this happens much less frequently than I'd like to admit; most Sundays, I'm thankful we can find clean clothes to wear—and that's ok. We're called to be holy, not to be color coordinated. But each of these small steps helps bring us a bit closer to Christ and may even help us become bit holier too.

Invitation to Ponder

Can you think of someone who lives, celebrates, and honors the Church's feast days and/or the changing liturgical seasons? How do you think this benefits them? Their friends and family? Do you think it would do the same for you?

_____

_____

_____

_____

_____

_____

_____

_____

_____

_____

_____

_____

_____

_____

Connecting to Scripture

PRAYER TO THE HOLY SPIRIT BEFORE READING SCRIPTURE

Come, Holy Spirit. Fill me with every grace and blessing necessary to understand the message prepared for and awaiting me in the Scriptures. May I grow deeper in faith, in hope, and in love with Jesus as I spend this time with the Word of God. Amen.

Matthew 15:4–10 _____

_____

_____

2 Thessalonians 2:15 _____

_____

_____

9 1 Corinthians 5:7–8 _____

_____

_____

9 1 Corinthians 11:1–2 _____

_____

_____

9 1 Corinthians 11:26 _____

_____

_____

Scripture Reflection

You're not just seeking him—he is also seeking you. For me, this is such a beautiful reminder that it's not me just wandering through the wilderness, calling out Jesus' name and hoping he responds. Sharing with Jesus this desire for closeness is what brings me—and you—to this study. Together, we've opened the door by taking time out of our busy schedules to grow. Do you know what happens when you open that door just a crack? Christ throws it wide open, because he is so happy to have you here. Celebrating the liturgical year is a way to find

God. As you celebrate, let him reveal himself to you. He is thrilled to have your heart!

There is a beautiful song lyric, "you are mine and I am yours." Celebrating the liturgical year faithfully, in all its richness and traditions, unites us with our Creator. It nourishes the soul. Just as that warm cup of coffee (or three) fuels our morning, celebrating our faith fuels our hearts and warms our souls. It gives us an intentional way to grow in holiness all year long.

Traditions have always been a part of Christianity, and Scripture encourages us not only to continue them, but to "stand firm and hold fast to the traditions that you were taught" (2 Thessalonians 2:15). Saint Paul doesn't say, "Sure, go ahead and do that if you want," or "Eh, skip Sunday Mass if you're tired." He tells us to stand firm and hold fast to these traditions so that Our Lord and God may strengthen our hearts in all that we do. He again tells us, "Be imitators of me, as I am of Christ. I praise you because you remember me in everything and hold fast to the traditions, just as I handed them on to you" (1 Corinthians 11:1–2). He lauds our efforts to maintain not only what we read but also what we witness in living out our Catholic faith. Blessings come to our families as we continue the traditions of our faith, passed down to us from generation to generation.

Let's Eat: Celebrations at the Dinner Table

Many of the cultural and religious traditions my family celebrates have food at their center. Have you ever noticed that no matter how removed we are from our countries of origin, we still stay connected to them via food? Some of my favorite family foods that go along with our faith traditions include Easter paska bread, baked paczki at the start of Lent, butter lambs with Easter brunch, and cinnamon rolls for Advent. I can almost smell them! Just thinking about these treats awakens my senses and memories.

The Catholic faith's greatest celebration, the Eucharist, is a meal of thanksgiving that doesn't symbolize but actually re-presents Jesus' sacrificial gift for each of us. Each Mass provides opportunities to have our senses awakened and our hearts filled with gratitude. At the core of all we do should be the memory of Jesus' sacrifice, giving our faith traditions depth of meaning and bringing us further along our journey to holiness: "For as often as you eat this bread and drink the cup, you proclaim the death of the Lord until he comes" (1 Corinthians 11:26).

Do you have family traditions that serve as markers throughout the liturgical year? It's never too late to take that very first step in starting some. Now, does this mean that a family who celebrates every feast day and holy day is more sanctified than the family that doesn't? Absolutely not. Remember, Jesus cares more about the intentions *behind* our celebration than *how* we celebrate or commemorate a day.

Creating Moments at Home

Women seem to have been created with an innate yearning for a life that cohesively brings together our spiritual, physical, and emotional needs. We are designed, as Saint Teresa Benedicta writes, "to cherish, guard, [and] protect ..."[3] As we live our lives liturgically, we are creating cherished memories not only for ourselves but also for our families and friends, while at the same time guarding and preserving the faith and traditions of generations past.

You Do You

As you read through this book, ask yourself, "How can I grow and share in God's glory with myself, my family, and those around me?"

One word of caution, though. As you read, please don't see this as a thousand new to-dos for your already-stuffed planner. How you decide to incorporate a season, feast day, or holy day into your life should uplift your spirit and spark your faith, not leave you exhausted.

I share this as it's something I'm continually working on. I'll never forget the year I crammed way too much into the days leading up to Easter. I arranged for my sister to come out to visit, planned egg hunts with a friend who was moving away, baked hot cross buns and paska bread from scratch three mornings in a row, prepared countless activities for my young son, scrubbed down the house in anticipation of Easter brunch … and that's just the beginning of the list.

Come Easter Sunday, I wasn't rejoicing in our Lord's resurrection; I was rejoicing that I didn't have twenty things to do that day. In retrospect, I would have done well to heed St. Paul's advice: "Clear out the old yeast, so that you may become a fresh batch of dough, inasmuch as you are unleavened. For our paschal lamb, Christ, has been sacrificed. Therefore let us celebrate the feast, not with the old yeast, the yeast of malice and wickedness, but with the unleavened bread of sincerity and truth" (1 Corinthians 5:7–8).

I had lost the freshness that I should have had and was an old, dry pile of yeast. Worn out, snappy, and downright exhausted was not the way to celebrate the resurrection of my Lord and Savior. I had lost sight of the meaning behind my family's traditions and celebrations and let them take the place that God should have had in my heart. Matthew 15:6 warns of this: "You have nullified the word of God for the sake of your tradition." While I certainly hope I didn't nullify his word, I definitely didn't put him first.

Can I add a second word of caution? We all have a friend or family member that we may try to emulate. But we are all created with our own uniqueness. As we read in 1 Corinthians 12, where would the body be if we were all a single member? What richness would be lost, and what expectations introduced if we all tried to be the same? Truly, we are each chosen and endowed as God sees fit with the gifts and talents unique to each of us. It's up to us to discover and share them.

Contemplate the Celebration

1. What does the phrase "living liturgically" mean to you? To your family?

_____

_____

_____

_____

_____

_____

_____

_____

_____

_____

_____

2. What talents do you have? How can you use those talents to live more in tune with the liturgical calendar?

_____

_____

_____

_____

_____

_____

_____

_____

_____

_____

3. Share a tradition your family celebrates, whether secular or religious. How can you use this tradition to draw closer to Christ?

_____

_____

_____

_____

_____

_____

_____

_____

_____

Closing Prayer

Heavenly Father, as I conclude this introduction to the liturgical year, I am so excited about the many new ways I can connect with you, the Church, and my family. May we strengthen each other in faith and love through these celebrations and traditions and ultimately draw ever closer to you.

I'm intrigued by how I can emulate Mary and Joseph, sharing and passing down Catholic traditions to my family, and make living liturgically an integral part of my life. How amazing you are to provide so many ways to keep my faith alive, vibrant, and relevant—a rich, fulfilling faith not just saved for Sundays but held close, day after day, enriching my life.

Lord, I promise not to get overwhelmed by the many ideas and suggestions presented in this book. Remembering that we are all created uniquely, with our own gifts and talents, I will rejoice in what my heart feels inspired to tackle and never feel guilty about what it does not. Living a more active life of faith is not a competition but a gift of joy to savor.

Invigorate my faith by the power of the Holy Spirit as I continue this study, reflecting on the liturgical year, the Scriptures, and the questions to ponder. May each chapter draw me closer and closer to you. Amen.

2: Advent

MAKE EVERY DAY BLESSED

Opening Prayer

Heavenly Father, the Advent season should be one filled with joy; however, you know how busy I can become with the details of Christmas. You have seen me making lists and checking them twice, as I fulfill my Santa duties. How often have I remembered to keep Christ in my pre-Christmas activities and celebrations?

Advent is a time of waiting in joyous anticipation of the coming of Christ—not only as an infant in Bethlehem, but also as the triumphant king in the Second Coming. The season is for preparing our hearts, minds, and homes for receiving Jesus. Do my Advent traditions reflect this vital aspect of the season?

Father, as I begin this next chapter, please open my mind and heart to receive the gifts that await me on these pages. Help me to pay close attention to the real reason for the season and the ways I can bless my family by incorporating the Church's rich traditions into our own.

Thank you for your unfailing love and the endless opportunities each liturgical season offers for me to grow in my faith. Thank you for unfathomable graces that are always calling me into deeper relationship with you. Thank you for your faithful promise to draw closer to me, as I draw closer to you. May every page of this study bring me one step nearer to you. Amen.

On My Heart

_____

_____

_____

_____

_____

_____

_____

_____

_____

_____

_____

_____

_____

_____

_____

_____

_____

Celebrating the Season of Advent

When I was a child, the arrival of the Advent season meant that Christmas was almost here! It meant creamy hot cocoa with crispy buttered crackers, glossy toy catalogs with pages that crinkled as they turned, snow-filled playdates with neighborhood friends in the brisk winter air, and the sugary joy of chocolate Advent calendars as we counted down the days to Christmas.

I loved Advent as a child would, in its purest and simplest form. It was a time filled with joy, excitement, and longing for Christmas Day. Each year, my parents drove my sister, brother, and me to our grandparents' house, where the familiar smells of traditional foods filled the air. The celebration began on Christmas Eve. Aunts, uncles, and cousins arrived throughout the day in preparation for the Christmas Eve meal that night. After dinner, we all gathered in the cozy living room and opened the ever-growing pile of sparkling, shiny presents gathered underneath the tree. While the deeper, more spiritual meaning of Advent wouldn't manifest itself until my adult years, the knowledge that something was coming—something extra special—was always there.

The word *Advent* means "coming," and is derived from the Latin word *adventus.* The Greek equivalent is *parousia*, which refers to the Second Coming of Christ. While most of us will probably never see the Second Coming of Christ here on earth (though we will in heaven!), we have the chance to celebrate his first coming each year on Christmas. Think about it! We have the opportunity, every single year, to celebrate the Son of God coming down from heaven to be among us and to live as one of us. Wow!

I think back to all the celebrations I've planned through the years. The hours spent on Pinterest sorting through decorating ideas, determining the right mix of guests, cleaning the house and scrubbing out cabinets in case they get opened—there was always so much intentionality behind each task to make sure the celebration was just right.

That is where Advent comes in. The celebration of the Incarnation—the fact that the Son of God took on human flesh (*Catechism*, 461)—isn't just any celebration; it's *the* celebration. To get ready for such a time, we have four weeks to prepare our hearts, making room in them, not just for Christmas Day but for the day Jesus returns to us here on earth.

The Season of Advent

Advent is the time leading up to Christmas Day. The length of Advent varies each year because the first day of Advent isn't fixed. And it doesn't always start on December 1, regardless of what the chocolate Advent calendars say!

So why does the first day of Advent change each year? According to the *General Norms for the Liturgical Year and the Calendar,* Advent begins on the Sunday falling on or closest to November 30.[4] In a given year, this can range from November 27 to December 3.

November 30 is the feast day of St. Andrew the Apostle, the very first of Jesus' disciples. Each year on November 30, many of my friends begin a novena called the St. Andrew Christmas Novena, sometimes simply referred to as "The Christmas Novena" because it ends on Christmas Eve. Unlike a traditional novena prayed over the course of nine days, this novena prayer lasts through all four weeks of Advent! For my friends and many others, this novena is a wonderful way to begin the Advent season with a focus on anticipation, penance, and prayer.

The first day of Advent also marks the start of the Church year. As the Church's liturgical year is cyclical, the events we celebrate throughout the year follow a chronological order: it starts with the birth of Christ and chronologically follows key events in his life. So the next time you're at the grocery store, pick up two bottles of champagne to celebrate both new years—the start of the Church's new liturgical year at the beginning of Advent and the secular New Year's Day on January 1 (introduced by Pope Gregory XIII in 1582 as part of the Gregorian calendar). Cheers!

With the start of the new Church year at the beginning of Advent, we also start a new lectionary cycle, which means that we'll hear different readings at Sunday Mass than we did during the previous year. Over the course of each year, we make our way through one of the synoptic Gospels (Matthew, Mark, and Luke) with portions of the Gospel of John read on special days. During Ordinary Time, the first reading, generally drawn from the Old Testament, relates to the theme of the Gospel. You can challenge your family to find the connection between the two readings, a practice that will reveal new insights into the Scriptures.

In our home, we have a large driftwood picture frame that holds beautiful, handmade Scripture art designed by some of my favorite Catholic artisans. I love to rotate the artwork throughout the year, and I've been increasingly focusing on inserting Scriptures from that year's Gospel. This gives us a chance to encounter the Word of God in the course of each day.

Visible Signs That Advent Is Here

As a little girl, one of the things I remember most vividly about the start of Advent (besides the chocolates inside our Advent calendar) is the colors in the Church as they changed from the green of Ordinary Time to the richest, most gorgeous shade of purple. While the purple of Lent symbolizes penitence, it has a different significance during Advent, when it emphasizes preparation for the coming of the Messiah.[5] Purple is the color of sovereignty and royalty, and it is displayed during Advent to show that we are anticipating the arrival of our King.

I love trying to coordinate my "Sunday best" with the liturgical colors, so I am grateful when we take a break from all the purple for the Third Sunday of Advent. (I only have so much purple in my wardrobe!) On the Third Sunday of Advent, also known as Gaudete Sunday, the liturgical colors change from purple to rose. The joyful rose color is inspired by the entrance antiphon sung at the start of the Mass that day. The antiphon, taken from Philippians 4:4, reads, "Rejoice in the Lord always. I shall say it again: rejoice!" (The Latin word *gaudete* means "rejoice.") Indeed, we rejoice in reaching the halfway point of Advent; the birth of Our Savior is near! At home, we mark this joyful Sunday with strawberry ice cream sundaes; the pink and rose in the ice cream bring the rose color from the Mass to our kitchen table. The sweetness of this frosty treat is just a taste of the celebration to come on Christmas Day.

One of the most beautiful traditions of Advent is the lighting of an Advent wreath. The wreath itself is a circle, symbolizing the perfect eternity of God; just like the circle, God has no beginning or end. Each week, we light one of the four candles; the three purple candles and one rose candle mirror the colors seen at Mass. Notice, though, that other decor is kept to a minimum in the Church because the sparkle of Christmas is not yet at hand.

The Blessed Virgin Mary

The Blessed Virgin Mary plays an especially prominent role during Advent—and why not? Who else experiences expectation as keenly as a pregnant woman? And who else would have anticipated the coming of the Messiah in the same way as the one who carried him in her womb for nine months? Her time of preparation becomes a model for those of us who follow in her footsteps during Advent.

During Advent, the liturgy of the Church "recalls the women of the Old Testament who prefigured and prophesied [Mary's] mission; it exalts her faith and the humility with which she promptly and totally submitted to God's plan of salvation; it highlights her presence in the events of grace preceding the birth of the Saviour. Popular piety also devotes attention to the Blessed Virgin Mary during Advent, as is evident from the many pious exercises practised at this time, especially the novena of the Immaculate Conception and of Christmas."[6]

The Feast of the Immaculate Conception highlights Mary's role in God's plan of salvation. This feast day is a holy day of obligation in the United States. While the feast is often misunderstood as celebrating Mary's conception of Jesus (which is actually marked on March 25 during the Feast of the Annunciation), it actually celebrates the doctrine that Mary was conceived without original sin. As Pope Pius IX proclaimed in 1854, "The most Blessed Virgin Mary was, from the first moment of her conception, by a singular grace and privilege of almighty God and by virtue of the merits of Jesus Christ, Savior of the human race, preserved immune from all stain of original sin" (*Ineffabilis Deus*). The feast is especially appropriate for the season of Advent, because the grace of Mary's preservation from sin was a necessary preparation for her role as the mother of the Messiah. Just like Mary, we strive during Advent to purify our own hearts to better receive Christ in them at Christmas.

The Novena of the Immaculate Conception begins on November 30 and concludes on the feast day itself. For me, these nine days of prayer to the Blessed Mother create the perfect beginning to Advent, laying the spiritual groundwork for the welcoming of her son on Christmas Day.

Invitation to Ponder

Think back to what Advent meant to you as a child. Did you celebrate Advent? Was it a separate season in your home? Or did Christmas start as soon as Thanksgiving ended? How have your childhood experiences influenced the way you celebrate Advent today?

_____

_____

_____

_____

_____

_____

_____

_____

_____

_____

_____

_____

_____

_____

Connecting to Scripture

PRAYER TO THE HOLY SPIRIT BEFORE READING SCRIPTURE

Come, Holy Spirit. Fill me with every grace and blessing necessary to understand the message, prepared for and awaiting me, in the Scriptures. May I grow deeper in faith, in hope, and in love with Jesus as I spend this time with the Word of God. Amen.

❧ Isaiah 11:1–10 _____

_____

_____

❧ Hosea 10:12 _____

_____

_____

❧ Malachi 3:1–5 _____

_____

_____

❧ Matthew 24:42–44 _____

_____

_____

✐ James 5:7–8 _____

_____

_____

Scripture Reflection

Advent is a quiet time of longing. Thinking back, we remember how the Jews longed for a Messiah. We call to mind our own longing for forgiveness and salvation that only Our Savior can bring.

Learning to Wait

As an adult, I've learned—often the hard way—that true contentment is gained not by immediate gratification but by practicing patience and waiting. It can be hard to balance this in the world we live in. When we can purchase the latest must-have with just a click (coupled with free two-day shipping), the message is clear: the world does not want us to be content with what we have. It does not want us to wait.

Even now, I sit here slightly irritated. My husband and I have always shared a family Bible, yet lately, we both seem to be needing it at the same time. We agreed that picking up a second Bible for our family was the right move. After hours of searching online for just the right one, I found it; and I also found that it's out of stock for the next forty days! What? No! I don't want to wait! I feel my frustration and irritation rise and am reminded of the words of James 5:8: "You too must be patient." So I take a deep breath, pre-order the book, and thank God for this opportunity to practice patience and wait.

I've watched enough cooking shows to know how to make a good wine reduction sauce. My life (and I'd wager yours too) can be as full—and sometimes as heated—as that pot of sauce. If we heat the sauce and let the water boil away until all that is left is a flavorful reduction, we have found the real richness of the sauce. The weeks leading up to Christmas are often as full as that boiling pot of sauce: busy with gift buying, sale shopping, cookie decorating, gingerbread baking, and travel plan making. If we boil away all that excess, what remains is the essence of all that is good.

For me, that is Advent. It's about clearing away the excess, focusing on what is truly important, and waiting in anticipation for Jesus' birth. The second half of James 5:8 says, "Make your hearts firm, because the coming of the Lord is at hand." What an excellent opportunity we have each Advent as we prepare our hearts for what is to come!

Being Refined

Pope Francis has observed that in Advent, "We rediscover the beauty of all being on a journey ... across the paths of time."[7] Advent truly is a journey, one in which we prepare ourselves for an event that took place thousands of years ago: the birth of Christ. It's a beautiful time when we can each reassess our thoughts on trust and humility concerning God, for the two are intrinsically linked. Mary didn't just trust God; she trusted him with such humbleness that she put aside her wants and needs to consent to his will, even though she knew the path ahead would not be an easy one. I'm often guilty—especially when life gets busy—of putting my wants and needs ahead of kindness and humility. Sign up to donate a fresh batch of cookies at the bake sale? Sorry, I already have family in town for the holidays and can't bake one more thing. Add an extra $25 into the adopt-a-family basket? Gosh, I would ... but I have that mani-pedi scheduled before my husband's Christmas party.

> But who can endure the day of his coming?
>> Who can stand firm when he appears?
> For he will be like a refiner's fire,
>> like fullers' lye.
> He will sit refining and purifying silver,
>> and he will purify the Levites,
> Refining them like gold or silver,
>> that they may bring offerings to the Lord in righteousness.
>>>>> (Malachi 3:2–3)

When I read this excerpt from the prophet Malachi, I feel like the Levites, needing Christ to purify and refine my soul. I see my misplaced priorities, each a tarnish on my heart. I long for the refinement Christ's coming will bring, and I take the time to look deep inside. Would it be so hard to make a double batch of cookies and bring some to Mass this weekend? Will that overpriced pedicure even be visible beneath my snow boots? Until Christ comes, we must, as Hosea 10:12 says, "Sow for yourselves justice, reap the reward of loyalty; break up for yourselves a new field, for it is time to seek the LORD." We take the time during Advent to break up the fields in our own lives that have hardened, gone dry, or become neglected. Just as a farmer tends to his crops, we tend to aspects of our own lives as we seek the coming of Our Lord.

Home Traditions

Throughout the season of Advent, the Old Testament readings we hear at Mass trace the ways in which God prepared his people for the coming of the Anointed One, the Christ. In one of these readings, we hear the prophet Isaiah proclaim, "A shoot shall sprout from the stump of Jesse, and from his roots, a bud shall blossom" (Isaiah 11:1). Christians have long interpreted this prophecy as saying that the Christ would come from the line of Jesse's descendants. Jesse, you might recall, was the father of King David. How interesting that Isaiah would focus on the Messiah's descent coming from Jesse, the humble farmer, rather than David, the mighty king!

This single line of Scripture has evolved into a tangible Advent tradition celebrated by Christians worldwide: the Jesse Tree. A Jesse Tree is a tree (or a representation of a tree) tracing the story of salvation history from creation to the birth of Jesus. Simple symbols (such as, a rainbow, a lyre, a crown, etc.) are added to the tree, representing important historical events and figures from the Old Testament that each played a particular role in salvation history.

In our home, we've lovingly created a Jesse Tree of our own. Each day of Advent, starting on the first Sunday of Advent, we read a Scripture verse together as a family. Then we play a little game based on the reading and add the corresponding ornament to our Jesse Tree. For our family, this has become a fun, interactive, and educational opportunity for us to not only learn but also to come together and celebrate each day of the Advent season.

Our Jesse Tree has also been a way for me to learn about being prepared on the journey. Invariably, there are days that we don't have an opportunity to hang an ornament on the tree—or days that we just forget. For me, these moments are chances to tend to my field, clear away any needless excess, and start again the next day.

"Therefore, stay awake! For you do not know on which day your Lord will come" (Matthew 24:42). This line is a constant reminder that each day provides a chance to reawaken to living the life that each of us is called to lead.

Each Advent, we light the candles on our Advent wreath. Then, beginning on St. Lucy's feast day (December 13), our soft candle lighting is augmented with the lights from our Christmas tree. I remember the first Christmas after getting married; my husband wanted to decorate the Christmas tree as soon as we took down the Thanksgiving decorations, and I didn't want to have a tree in the living room until Christmas morning! We were able to compromise by putting up the Christmas tree on St. Lucy's feast day and decorating it with nothing more than simple twinkling white lights. On Christmas Eve, we add glittering tinsel, shiny glass balls, and colorful ornaments. Lucy, from the name Lucia, means light, and each year on her feast day during Advent, we celebrate her and the light she brings. We also thank her for the peace she brought to our marriage in helping us agree on when to put up and decorate the tree!

Contemplate the Celebration

1. Advent can be a time of rushed excess. Every day we are bombarded with so much to do, so much to buy, so much to make ... so much of everything. What areas do you recognize as excess, and how can you be more intentional about making Advent a season of preparation?

_____

_____

_____

_____

_____

_____

_____

_____

_____

_____

2. Reread Malachi 3:2-3 and Hosea 10:12. In what areas of your life do
   you feel God working to refine and purify? What fields do you have
   that need to be broken up and tilled again?

_____

_____

_____

_____

_____

_____

_____

_____

_____

_____

3. Advent is a time to prepare your heart and life for Jesus' coming.
   How can you extend the virtues and values of patience and preparation throughout the entire year?

_____

_____

_____

_____

_____

_____

_____

_____

_____

_____

_____

_____

4. Living Liturgically through Tradition: How does your family celebrate Advent? In what ways can you use your existing traditions to
   bring you closer to Christ?

_____

_____

_____

_____

_____

_____

_____

_____

_____

_____

Closing Prayer

Dear God, thank you for giving us time to ready ourselves for all the blessings the Christmas season brings. Thank you for the gift of Advent, your perfectly planned time of preparation and waiting.

So often we get caught up in the busyness of life, with an endless to-do list that seems to grow each day.

Thank you, Lord, for reminding me to take the time during Advent to break up the fields in my life that have hardened, gone dry, or become neglected. Just as a farmer tends to his crops, we need to tend to the many aspects of our lives (especially the spiritual) as we seek your coming.

The hustle and bustle of the holidays (or even the ordinary days) can often take root, cluttering the fields in our heart and our home. Help us to keep the coming of Your Son central in our lives as we strive each day to be ready to receive you when you come.

Thank you for reminding me in this chapter that we have the chance, every single year, to celebrate God coming to earth to be among us, to live as one of us! Thank you for offering a way to create a peaceful atmosphere within my heart and home, where I can say grace and remember that Christmas is coming—while never forgetting it isn't here yet. Amen.

3: Christmas

Opening Prayer

Lord, for so long I have celebrated Christmas in place of the joyous Advent season. I have inadvertently shortened my celebration of the twelve days of Christmas, often exhausted by the hustle and bustle of the month leading up to December 25. As I enter into this chapter, I long to learn about the actual Christmas season, which begins on Christmas Day and ends on the Feast of the Baptism of the Lord in mid-January.

I pray that my heart be opened to view many of the traditions we celebrate, especially those Christmas traditions begun many years ago, with a fresh perspective. I want to look anew at my family's wonderful traditions passed down from generation to generation. Lord, reveal the reasons behind our celebrations as they relate to my relationship with you.

By taking the time to learn the origins of our traditions, and by saving the celebrations until the season of Christmas, we can bring greater meaning and grow closer to Christ during this special time of year.

Thank you for your unfailing love and the endless opportunities to grow in my faith during Christmas. Thank you for your unfathomable love, which provides so many ways to grow in my relationship with you. As I draw closer to you, you promise to draw ever closer to me. May every page I read here bring me one step nearer to you. Amen.

On My Heart

_____

_____

_____

_____

_____

_____

_____

_____

_____

_____

_____

_____

_____

_____

_____

_____

Celebrating the Season of Christmas

Two thousand years ago, a tiny baby was born to a simple carpenter and his young wife. The couple, alone in an overcrowded town, sought shelter from the cold in a stable among the animals. There the baby was born—a tiny little boy who would one day save us from death.

We've spent the past four weeks of Advent preparing for Christmas Day. Like fine silver and gold, we've become refined and purified (or at least slightly less tarnished). Along with our family and friends, we are ready to celebrate Christ's Mass—Christmas—with hearts full of joy!

The Christmas Season

Christmas, a holy day of obligation, is celebrated on December 25. If you're like our neighbors, Christmas ends the very next day: the stockings taken down, the wreath packed away, and the dried-out tree—up since Thanksgiving—tossed out to the curb. For Catholics, though, the fun has just begun. In the Catholic faith, Christmas isn't just a single day; it's an entire season that lasts for more than two weeks!

The liturgical season of Christmas begins with the vigil Masses on Christmas Eve and runs through the Feast of the Baptism of the Lord, which falls on the Sunday following the Feast of the Epiphany on January 6. Like Advent, the length of the Christmas season varies from year to year, depending on which day of the week Christmas falls.

Special feast days, plus a smattering of secular holidays, punctuate the entire season. In our home, we treat Christmas like a birthday party that never ends! Some of the principal feasts we celebrate during the Christmas season include:

⑦ **Feast of the Nativity of the Lord** (December 25).

⑦ **Feast of St. Stephen**, first Christian martyr (December 26). In certain countries, this is also Boxing Day, the day when the alms boxes at church were traditionally opened and the money given to the poor and also when household servants received gifts from their employers.

⑦ **Feast of St. John the Evangelist** (December 27). St. John's Gospel has its own nativity narrative that focuses on Jesus' divine origins.

⑦ **Feast of the Holy Innocents** (December 28). This is the day on which we remember the massacre of young children in Bethlehem by King Herod in his attempt to kill Jesus. We also pray for all children killed by genocide and abortion.

⑦ **Feast of the Holy Family** (varies; Sunday in the octave of Christmas). This day is a time for Christian families to rededicate themselves to the familial example of Joseph, Mary, and Jesus.

⑦ **New Year's Eve** (December 31). This holiday is celebrated in many places with extended exposition of the Eucharist, the singing of the *Te Deum*, and prayer vigils giving thanks for the previous year and dedicating the new year to the Lord (see the *Directory on Popular Piety and the Liturgy,* 114).

⑦ **Solemnity of the Blessed Virgin Mary, the Mother of God, and the Octave Day of Christmas** (January 1). The Church also marks this date as the World Day of Peace, on which the pope releases a message of peace for the whole world.

⮑ **Optional Memorial of the Holy Name of Jesus** (January 3). This is the day when Jesus was brought to the Temple and officially named.

⮑ **Twelfth Night** (January 5). Although not found on the Church's liturgical calendar, this holiday was long celebrated as the eve of Epiphany with special food and the exchange of gifts.

⮑ **Epiphany** (traditionally January 6, but now celebrated in the United States on the Sunday between January 2 and 8). This feast marks the coming of the Magi and the epiphany, or revelation, of the Lord to the whole world. It is traditionally celebrated with the blessing of the home and expressions of hospitality to strangers.

⮑ **The Feast of the Baptism of the Lord** (the Sunday after Epiphany). This closes the season of Christmas and offers a great opportunity for families to remember their own baptisms.

The *Directory on Popular Piety and the Liturgy* notes with approval the many displays of popular piety that accompany the Christmas season. Those traditions best reflect "the richness and complexity of the mystery of the Lord's manifestation" when they are rooted in an authentic spirituality of the season. What characterizes the spirituality of Christmas?

⮑ *A "Spirituality of the Gift"* rooted in the gift of the Christ child, given to us out of God's infinite love for us.

The practice of solidarity with the poor, inspired by God's solidarity with sinners in the event of the Incarnation.

A reverence for the sacredness of all human life, inspired by the fact that the Son of God chose to be born into the world as a vulnerable little child.

The practice of joy and peace, inspired by the joyful message of the angels proclaiming, "peace on earth to men of good will" (Luke 2:14).

A "spirit of simplicity and poverty, humility and trust in God."

Finally, the Church urges us to keep the mystery of Christ's birth at the center of our traditions and celebrations "so as to ensure that the strong religious tradition surrounding Christmas is not secularized by consumerism."[8]

Christmas Traditions

In sixth grade, I left Catholic school and enrolled in the new public middle school near our home. I remember feeling more than a bit of shock that first year. Gone were the uniforms, morning prayer, and a sense of belonging. Just before Thanksgiving, I made my first real friend, a sweet girl named Jane, who had recently emigrated from China. All we could talk about was Christmas—or, at least, that's all I could talk about. As I shared the plans I had for the upcoming break, she interrupted me with a slightly disgusted one-two punch: "We don't celebrate Christmas or some baby that supposedly has superpowers. We also don't kill trees."

I stood there, quite dumbfounded. I said nothing because I had no idea how to answer her misguided—yet deeply profound—question: Why did we do the things we do?

So many of the traditions we observe, especially those of Christmas, started many years ago. While the traditions are passed down from generation to generation, the reasons we follow them are often lost. Let's look at some of those traditions and how they first started.

Visible Signs That Christmas Is Here

Do you put up a Christmas tree in your home? Christmas trees, or evergreen trees, have been a symbol of everlasting life since ancient times.

My grandfather and my aunt were both career employees of the U. S. Postal Service. They were fond of the old saying, "Not rain, nor sleet, nor snow, nor hail can ever stop us from delivering your mail." Much like a postal worker, the evergreen tree remains steadfast regardless of the weather. This symbol of everlasting life lives in some of the harshest conditions, and even in below-zero temperatures, it doesn't die.

While the exact origin of the Christmas tree isn't known, a popular legend says that it started with Saint Boniface.[9] Born in 680, he chopped down an oak tree worshiped by German pagans. In its place, a small fir tree grew. Saint Boniface used the tree to bring Christianity to the Germans; the triangular shape of the tree points to heaven, its three sides represent the Trinity, and the evergreen qualities of the tree exemplify the everlasting life that Jesus brings.

A second popular legend is that the modern-day Christmas tree originated from the medieval mystery plays.[10] These plays took place in the town square on the feast day of Adam and Eve, December 24. On stage sat a tree, decorated with apples representing the forbidden fruit, wafers representing the Eucharist, and candles representing the light of Christ. The candles also brightened up the stage during those dark medieval nights! The Christmas trees of today are very much the same, albeit with a less flammable and less edible twist: the candles have been replaced with strings of lights, and the apples with shiny red glass balls.

While our homes and churches are often decorated in red and green, the vestments worn by the clergy are a brilliant white. The white clerical robes are mirrored in the white Christ Candle; placed in the center of the Advent wreath, the candle is lit on Christmas Day, indicating Christmastide has arrived.

The universality of the Catholic Church—its openness to all peoples—is wonderfully expressed during the Feast of the Epiphany. Every year in our parish, we set up a large manger scene during the last week of Advent. Then, on Christmas Day, baby Jesus appears in the crib. Over the course of the next twelve days, the three Magi travel throughout the church as they slowly make their way to the nativity scene. The children of the parish love hunting for the Magi, to see where they'll turn up each day on their journey!

There are so many more ways that we as a collective Catholic community celebrate Christmas each year. Our families, friends, ethnicities, cultures, and geographic locations all influence the way we bring Christ into our homes. By taking the time to learn the origins of our traditions and saving the celebrations until the true season of Christmas, we have the opportunity to find greater meaning in this special time of year and grow closer to Christ.

Invitation to Ponder

Make a list of the many ways you celebrate. Do you know why they're part of your annual traditions? Take the time to find out. What role does Christ's birth play in your celebrations and traditions?

_____

_____

_____

_____

_____

_____

_____

_____

_____

_____

_____

Connecting to Scripture

PRAYER TO THE HOLY SPIRIT BEFORE READING SCRIPTURE

Come, Holy Spirit. Fill me with every grace and blessing necessary to understand the message, prepared for and awaiting me, in the Scriptures. May I grow deeper in faith, in hope, and in love with Jesus as I spend this time with the Word of God. Amen.

⌐ Isaiah 7:14 _____

_____

_____

⌐ Psalm 112:6-8_____

_____

_____

⌐ Luke 1:26-38, 46-47 _____

_____

_____

⌐ Luke 2:1-7_____

_____

_____

⌐ Luke 2:8-16 _____

_____

_____

Scripture Reflection

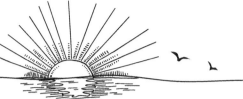

In December 2015, *National Geographic* published an article titled "How the Virgin Mary Became the World's Most Powerful Woman." Amazingly, Mary is one of the women most frequently featured on the cover of *Time* magazine since it began publication in 1923. Like Beyoncé, Shakira, and Cher, she is known throughout the world by just her first name. She is the Mother of God.

Jesus had been the focus of my faith life since childhood. My high school youth group friends and I all knew we could "find a friend in Jesus." Mary seemed far off, a quiet mention on the periphery of the Scriptures. She was larger than life, yet not a focus in mine.

In my mid-thirties, I joined a women's Bible study with one of my best friends. While we covered many biblical stories during the yearlong study, it was the announcement of the Incarnation of Jesus, brought to Mary by the archangel Gabriel at the Annunciation that began my relationship with Mary. In Luke 1:26–38, the angel Gabriel visits and greets Mary: "Hail, favored one! The Lord is with you."

It was her initial response that touched me: she was "greatly troubled" and "pondered what sort of greeting this might be." To have an angel suddenly appear in your room, telling you that God thinks you're a big deal … I can't even imagine how "greatly troubled" she must have felt!

Then, in the next moment, the angel told her to not be afraid, and, suddenly, she wasn't. Her faith was so strong that she let go of her fears and opened her heart to God's plan. No questions asked, no bargaining with God, no urgent rush to call a friend. Nothing—except complete trust in God and consent to do his will.

A few years ago, a different friend casually mentioned to a group of us that her husband was heading to the doctor's office the next day because he hadn't been feeling well. Toni wasn't very concerned, and we all laughed about how our husbands were always trying to avoid going to see the doctor! The following day, she called with an update: his aches and pains were advanced kidney cancer, and it had metastasized to his bones and lungs. I remember quietly sitting down on the couch in utter disbelief. We were both young couples, just starting our families. How could this be happening?

Throughout the next year of his life, Toni remained his rock. She continually prayed for a miracle, and, when it became clear that one would not come, she prayed for peace and strength. Her husband passed away fourteen months after the initial diagnosis. Her trust in God throughout that time never faltered. Like Mary, she committed herself to quietly accepting the role put before her, knowing that she would never have the answers she sought here on earth. She found solace in knowing God was by her side through it all.

Isaiah 7:14 says, "Therefore the Lord himself will give you a sign; the young woman, pregnant and about to bear a son, shall name him Emmanuel." *Emmanuel* means "God is with us," and Isaiah's prophecy was fulfilled on that first Christmas. Since that day, God has, indeed, been with us through our highs and our lows, our moments of renewal and our moments of doubt, our moments of joy and our moments of trouble.

Think of a time when you received news that greatly troubled you. Did you trust from the start that, no matter the outcome, God was with you? Psalm 112:6–8 tells us to have a heart that "is tranquil, without fear" and that we should never "fear an ill report." Just as Mary let go of her fears and trusted God to walk by her side through whatever would come, we, too, can find peace and strength when life takes an unexpected or devastating turn.

Making Do with What We've Got

When I was pregnant with our first child, I went into planning mode. We took birth classes as a couple and researched the top hospitals in our area. My husband and I read articles about how to prepare for childbirth, loaded up the iPod with calming meditations for what we anticipated would be twelve hours of active labor, and even wrote up a detailed birth plan, complete with the outfits (organic cotton only, please) and blankets that would first touch our baby's soft skin.

If Mary had made her own birth plan, it probably didn't include a long trip via donkey in her ninth month of pregnancy or giving birth in a stable. There was no hospital room to rest in, no midwife to assist her during birth. There was no recovery room to rest in, and nothing but a feeding trough in which to lay her newborn baby. Luke 2:7 says, "She wrapped him in swaddling clothes and laid him in a manger, because there was no room for them in the inn." Even in these conditions, Mary didn't say a word. Scripture doesn't say she made a scene at the innkeeper's door, or complained to Joseph that he should have made hotel arrangements before their arrival, or shouted out to God in anger and frustration at the situation. She quietly made do with what she had, and that was that. For me, her quiet resilience is a character-istic I admire and try to emulate—and one I seem to have the oppor-tunity to practice every day.

Food for Our Souls

The encounters with angels that we hear about during the Christmas season leave me with the distinct impression that, far from being a quiet, calm experience, it was a bit unnerving. Mary was "greatly troubled" by her encounter with the angel Gabriel, and the shepherds were "struck with great fear" when angels appeared to them announcing the birth of Christ (Luke 2:9). In both instances, the angels' words were reassuring, advising Mary and the shepherds not to be afraid.

These two instances share something else in common. The angels appeared and brought their message not to great kings and Pharisees but to ordinary, everyday people—people just like you and me. I've often wondered what the shepherds thought when they met the Holy Family, or why the angels shared the message with them—mere shepherds—in the first place. Was it that the angels were so excited to share the news that they shouted it out to the first people they encountered? Or was there a reason that the shepherds were chosen to be the first recipients of the Good News?

Perhaps it was the simplicity of the shepherds that made them perfect to be the first to look upon Jesus in the manger, allowing them to understand the true meaning of what lay before them. The shepherds would have been well acquainted with the purpose of a manger: to provide animals with their daily nourishment. For us, what lies in the manger isn't food to satisfy the physical longings of our bodies but nourishment for our souls. It's a never-ending source of food for our souls; we are fed abundantly by God's Word, the sacraments, the saints, the rosary, and the Mass. Every day we have the opportunity, much like the animals in the stable, to feast and be filled.

Home Traditions

As a child, my family used to pile into the minivan every December 23 and drive two hours through the snow-covered Pocono Mountains to my grandparents' house. We are of Polish and Slovak descent, so Christmas was always celebrated at sundown on Christmas Eve—a common tradition of Eastern Europeans. The beautifully decorated tables sparkled with grandma's fine china and silver; the sweet smell of nut roll, lobster, and browned butter permeated the air, and the warm feeling of family filled every space in the room. Together with all our aunts, uncles, and cousins, we feasted on old-world dishes as the magic of Christmas filled our hearts.

Time passed and roles changed, and now we are the adults surrounded by young children. We continue many of the same traditions I knew as a child: We celebrate the start of Christmas on Christmas Eve, and the table is filled with many of the same dishes our family has prepared for generations. And the traditions of my family have blended with those of my husband's family: Fresh crab sits beside the lobster each Christmas Eve, and the smell of warm cinnamon rolls fills the house each Christmas morning.

Our Christmas celebration now extends well past Christmas Day. Along with many of our friends, we've been making a conscious effort to celebrate the entire season of Christmastide. At home, we start our mornings with a Twelve Days of Christmas calendar; like an Advent calendar, tasty chocolate sits inside each of the twelve pockets as we mark the days of the season. One of my good friends hosts a "favorite things" party for us ladies, and we have such fun sharing and swapping our most recommended items with one another!

Christmas is the one time of year we all feel a bit like children—and that's such a good thing. Saint Thérèse of Lisieux wrote that "only little children, and those who are like them, will be admitted to the heavenly banquet." Does this mean we should get caught up in the gift-receiving, commercialism, and consumerism of the season? No, but we, instead, strive to get caught up in the excitement of the gift we all celebrate and receive on Christmas Day: the gift that Jesus brings.

Contemplate the Celebration

1. Like Mary and the shepherds in the field, we have times when we are greatly troubled. God's message is clear: Be not afraid, and trust in him instead. Armed with this knowledge, what will you do differently the next time your heart is troubled?

_____

_____

_____

_____

_____

_____

_____

_____

_____

2. Whether it's the latest Christmas, semi-annual, or year-end sale, the message of needing something more is always there. We're pushed to have the newest fashion, to live in a bigger home, to drive a better car, to follow the latest diet fad. In what area in your

life do you feel you're always striving to achieve more? Just as Mary found contentment in God, what can you let go of to find peace in your life?

_____

_____

_____

_____

_____

_____

_____

_____

_____

3. God routinely chooses not the wealthiest or most powerful to receive his messages, but, rather, he turns to ordinary people: the shepherds, a carpenter, a young girl. How does knowing that God chooses the everyday person impact the way you see his love for you? Your love for others? Your love for yourself?

_____

_____

_____

_____

_____

_____

_____

_____

4. Living liturgically through tradition: Think of the traditions your family observes during the Christmas season. Do you find pleasure in these traditions, or do they feel like "one more thing" during the busy holiday season? What traditions do you want to carry forward this year, and in what ways can you use these existing traditions to bring you closer to Christ?

_____

_____

_____

_____

_____

_____

_____

_____

_____

Closing Prayer

Dear Lord, I thank you today for the simple things in life—the shining stars, the wind in the trees, the natural wonders all around us. Each day, I wake up knowing—much like the newborn babe—that I have a fresh start, a new beginning. Every year as we celebrate the birth of Our Savior, Jesus Christ, I am reminded of the simplicity and wonder you place within my own life.

Prominent in the Christmas story is the Blessed Virgin Mother. Her fiat should also be celebrated—what a model of faith, trust, and the power

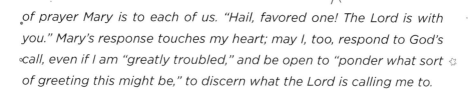

of prayer Mary is to each of us. "Hail, favored one! The Lord is with you." Mary's response touches my heart; may I, too, respond to God's call, even if I am "greatly troubled," and be open to "ponder what sort of greeting this might be," to discern what the Lord is calling me to.

Like the shepherds, may I, also, be simple, humble, and ready to receive the Lord's blessing.

Invigorate my faith by the power of the Holy Spirit as I continue to reflect on the liturgical year, the Scriptures, and the questions to ponder. May each chapter draw me closer and closer to you. Amen.

4: Lent

MAKE EVERY DAY BLESSED

Opening Prayer

Lord, the season of Lent calls for me to step away from the whirlwind that is my daily life and offers me the opportunity to focus, even if just for a few weeks, on my relationship with you. Lent is a time to pay more attention to prayer, charity, and fasting. Help me learn how to maximize the spiritual benefits of a Lent well lived, one beyond just avoiding chocolate.

Lord, guide me in developing better habits for time spent with you. Please allow my prayer time and reading of the Scriptures to be more meaningful while I spend less time indulging my vices and temptations.

Lent is a quiet, penitent time for me to grow through prayer, self-sacrifice, and caring for others. Heavenly Father, open my heart to see how you want me to grow in each of these three ways. So much of my life feels like one day of exhaustion after the next; help me to let go of all the excess, creating room for you and your wondrous love.

Thank you for your merciful love and for providing this amazing prayerful time each year to grow in my faith.

I am in awe every time I gaze upon the cross and contemplate the sacrifice, obedience, and unconditional love that put you there. As I draw closer to you on the cross, may I feel the love you have for me. May every page in this study bring me one step nearer to you. Amen.

On My Heart

_____

_____

_____

_____

_____

_____

_____

_____

_____

_____

_____

_____

_____

_____

_____

_____

_____

_____

Celebrating the Season of Lent

Do you look forward to the season of Lent? I do. With the bustle of Christmas long behind me and the new year—with all its potential—inspiring new goals and aspirations, Lent brings a sense of quiet calm and peace. Lent is a season for us, as Christians, to focus our lives on penitential acts as we prepare for the Resurrection celebration to come on Easter Sunday.

Have you noticed that, unlike Christmas, which occurs on December 25 every single year, Lent and Easter have no fixed celebration dates on the calendar? Lent begins on Ash Wednesday and ends at the start of the Mass of the Lord's Supper on Holy Thursday. The actual date of Ash Wednesday varies each year, though, and is determined by counting backward from Easter, which can fall any time between March 22 and April 25. Back in 325, the Council of Nicaea decided that Easter would always fall on the first Sunday following the first full moon after the spring equinox (known as the "paschal full moon"), and those dates are determined from tables rather than actual astronomical observations. Clear as mud, no?

If you're like me, you're probably wondering about the significance of the paschal full moon. According to the Jewish calendar, this is the day on which the Passover is celebrated every year. By coordinating Holy Week with the paschal full moon, the Church celebrates the events of Jesus' Passion, death, and resurrection under the same moon that Jesus would have. Pretty cool, huh?

Abstinence and Fasting

Let's talk about fasting and abstinence, Lenten practices that enable us to detach from the material and focus on our spiritual selves. When we do, we create space in our lives and hearts that God can fill with the goodness only he can bring.

Although many people give up something as a way of fasting throughout Lent, all the faithful are required to abstain from meat and fast on Ash Wednesday and Good Friday. On these days, we eat no more than one full meal and two smaller meals, both meatless. These two small meals may be consumed at regular mealtimes, as long as these two meals combined are still smaller than the full meal. Now, this doesn't mean we should make up for the size of the smaller meals by having a double serving of deep-dish veggie lasagna with cheesy garlic bread and salad as the main meal (though my husband has tried). The main meal itself should be of regular size, or the size you would normally prepare for yourself.[11]

In our home, we usually have toast with peanut butter for breakfast, a veggie burger and salad for lunch, and vegetable soup for dinner. Speaking of soup, one Lenten practice shared in recent years on social media has been a forty-day Lenten soup fast. Cooks become rather creative with soup recipes, which can be found all over Pinterest and are good meatless options for Fridays. The soup fast provides another innovative example of the many forms fasting may take.

Fasting isn't easy—nor is it meant to be. At my house, the next meal is readily available, and so are the ingredients for the entire week's meal plan. My fridge is packed with fresh meats and cheeses, the counters covered in baskets of fruits and vegetables, and my pantry loaded with canned and dry goods. Many Americans may miss breakfast rushing out the door in the morning or work late and be very hungry by the time they get through rush hour traffic, but thankfully most of us have no idea what it means to be truly hungry.

When the slightest hint of hunger appears, I often have an apple in my purse, a bar in my desk drawer, or a package of almonds in my gym bag. As a society, we are used to having our immediate needs met. When we fast, however, we delay gratification. It's an opportunity for us to practice a gift of the Holy Spirit: self-control. Richard Foster, in his book *Celebration of Discipline: The Path to Spiritual Growth,* wrote, "Our human cravings and desires are like rivers that tend to overflow their banks; fasting helps keep them in their proper channels."

Abstinence is a word commonly associated with fasting but has a separate meaning when it comes to our Lenten practices. Remember those veggie burgers we ate for lunch on Ash Wednesday and Good Friday? We also have them for lunch on most Fridays during Lent. That's because the Fridays of Lent, while not fasting days, are days when we're required to abstain from meat.

Fridays of Lent have turned into some of our favorite days; my husband is part of the Knights of Columbus at our church, so every Friday we dine at the parish fish fry. We join other families at the outdoor tables and have a wonderful time sharing a fish meal while the kids play and run around. Interestingly, it's often on these Friday nights that we become most aware of what others are sacrificing; I pass on dessert, a friend has water instead of wine, and some of the children even forgo ketchup on their fried fish sticks. Afterward, we come together to pray and meditate with the rest of our parish family in a Stations of the Cross service; our hearts (and tummies!) feel full long after the evening ends.

Ash Wednesday

A few years ago on Ash Wednesday, my husband sent me a picture he had taken in front of a large commercial shopping center. A pastor stood behind a large cardboard sign that read, "Lent Has Started: Get Your Ashes Here!" A line had formed beside the sign, each person waiting to receive ashes on their foreheads. We were both a bit taken aback—and then further surprised to learn that Ash Wednesday is not a holy day of obligation, nor are ashes required to be distributed only in a church.[12] Catholics are encouraged to attend Mass and receive ashes on our foreheads as a sign that we are entering into the penitential period of Lent.

When you receive ashes, you'll hear one of two phrases: "You are from dust, and to dust you shall return"; or "Turn away from sin and be faithful to the Gospel."[13] The first speaks directly to our mortality; no matter what we accomplish, what we have, or what we do in this life, our bodies are ultimately no more than dust. The second is a sober reminder of our need to repent and live a holy life. The ashes on our foreheads are an outward sign of our willingness to do that.

There is no set rule for how long you should leave the ashes on. Attitudes toward removal of the ashes seem to group people into one of two camps: those who let the ashes come off on their own and those who break out the soap and water right after Mass. For me, leaving the ashes on is an opportunity to do a bit of street evangelization. I remember when a woman in my Pilates class came to the gym wearing ashes; I had no idea Kim was Catholic! We ended up sharing which parishes we attended and found that we knew many of the same people across our communities. Even more importantly, we both had the opportunity to share the story of Ash Wednesday with several members of our class, who wanted to let Kim know she had a smudge on her forehead.

Kim inspired me to begin receiving my ashes at morning Mass and then go about my day without removing them. It's become a way for me to practice humility and courage; it takes a lot of both for me to walk around the grocery store with a black smear on my forehead. So many times, people will tell me how they remember receiving ashes as a child and how they should begin receiving them again, or (my favorite): "Oh my, is that today? I need to stop by the church!" It's become a way for me to share my faith by being a witness—in this case, without even saying a word.

Visible Signs That Lent Is Here

When my son was four years old, we walked into Mass on the first Sunday of Lent, and he happily announced, "Look, Mommy. It's Advent!" His confusion was understandable; many of the liturgical colors of Lent are like those of Advent. Purple or violet is the primary color of Lent (just as in Advent) because it traditionally represents penitence. It is also the color of mourning, often used during funeral masses. During Lent, we anticipate Christ's pain and suffering on the cross, knowing that the brilliant white of redemption is to come.[14]

We get a break from purple on the fourth Sunday of Lent, known as Laetare Sunday. The rose-colored vestments are a signal that we are midway through the Lenten season—a cause for rejoicing! In our home, we celebrate with delicious strawberry ice cream sundaes, just as we do for Gaudete Sunday during Advent.

Laetare Sunday receives its name from the Latin word for *rejoice*, which is the opening word of the antiphon sung at the beginning of Mass, taken from Isaiah 66:10:

> Rejoice with Jerusalem and be glad because of her,
>> all you who love her;
> Rejoice with her in her joy,
>> all you who mourn over her.

While we may still be in a penitential season of "mourning," the music, prayers, and readings of Laetare Sunday remind us of God's promise to rescue us from sin and death. As Pope John Paul II once said, "We are an Easter people, and Alleluia is our song!"[15]

Many Ways to Look at Fasting

Personal choices in fasting will be different for each of us. I'm not a foodie, caffeine addict, or sugar lover, so fasting from a particular food never felt like much of a sacrifice to me. I have been guilty of fasting from bread during Lent, knowing it would help me shed a few extra pounds. For me, this was the wrong choice for a personal fast because it did nothing to foster a closer relationship with Christ and, instead, only served my self-interests.

These past few years, after much discernment, I've found a way to truly fast from something I love while growing in faith and self-control. While I'm not a foodie, I am a bookie (of the literary sort, mind you, not the gambling kind). Each night before bed, I devour history and historical fiction, often reading well into the wee hours of the morning. During Lent, I fast from novels and replace them with books rich in the tradition of our faith—books by Bishop Robert Barron, Thomas Aquinas, Scott Hahn, Thérèse of Lisieux, and John Newman, to name just a few. It's a challenge for me! At the end of a long day, I want the escape that only getting lost in a story can bring. Reading these rich texts requires attention, patience, and focus—things I'm entirely out of by nightfall. But it's here that I find the beauty of Lent; in letting go of what I want and replacing it with Christ, I feel my heart opening, my mind stretching, and my will bending toward the Lord.

Invitation to Ponder

Think back to the things you've given up for Lent. What was your intention behind each fast? Were you sacrificing "that thing" because it provided an opportunity for you to grow in holiness or because it was in your self-interest? Does a nonfood option seem to be a better choice for your life? Consider planning for this coming Lent. What will you fast from, and, when you feel those cravings kick in, how will you turn to God?

_____

_____

_____

_____

_____

_____

_____

_____

_____

_____

_____

_____

_____

_____

Connecting to Scripture

PRAYER TO THE HOLY SPIRIT BEFORE READING SCRIPTURE

Come, Holy Spirit. Fill me with every grace and blessing necessary to understand the message, prepared for and awaiting me, in the Scriptures. May I grow deeper in faith, in hope, and in love with Jesus as I spend this time with the Word of God. Amen.

᜔ Deuteronomy 8:3 _____

_____

_____

᜔ Exodus 34:28 _____

_____

_____

᜔ Esther 4:16 _____

_____

_____

᜔ Acts 14:23 _____

_____

_____

ꟳ Isaiah 58:8–11 _____

_____

_____

ꟳ Matthew 4:1–4 _____

_____

_____

ꟳ John 3:30 _____

_____

_____

ꟳ James 5:16 _____

_____

_____

Scripture Reflection

Receiving ashes and practicing fasting creates space in our hearts, our minds, and even in our wallets so that we can seek and serve the

Lord more fully. Fasting, along with prayer and almsgiving, rounds out the set of magnificent tools offered by the Lord, and the Church, for our Lenten journey.

It's important to remember that it truly is a journey we are on. Like all journeys, there will be times when we are sailing on cruise control, and times when we hit every bump in the road. There will be times when we find opportunities to go above and beyond in our prayer life, and times when we remember it's Good Friday just moments after taking that last delicious bite of a double bacon cheeseburger (been there, done that). Much like a mantra, John 3:30 plays itself over in my head throughout Lent: "He must increase; I must decrease." Prayer, fasting, and almsgiving create an opportunity for us to do just that.

Prayer

I have a faith-filled friend who wakes up at 5 a.m. each day to pray the Rosary over a cup of coffee before her children wake up. She inspires me by her devotion. I tried it once and ended up a tired, hot mess for the rest of the day. James 5:16 says, "The fervent prayer of a righteous person is very powerful." I definitely did not feel righteous that day, and my weary morning prayers were less than fervent.

The right time to pray is different for each of us. With mornings out of the equation, the quiet of the night is the time when I find myself most open to having a conversation with God. During Lent, I add a single decade of the Rosary to my nighttime routine; it's a practice that makes my prayer time during Lent different—and, more importantly, deeper—than during other times of the year. I have a long way to go in becoming a righteous person of fervent prayer, but it's a start.

Fasting

Did you know there are more than seventy references to fasting in the Bible? Seventy! Fasting used to be an integral part of everyday life, practiced routinely in times of need. Before Moses wrote down the Ten Commandments given to him by God, he fasted for forty days and forty nights (Exodus 34:28). Esther asked her people to pray and fast for her before she went to the king (Esther 4:16). Paul and Barnabas fasted before appointing elders in the Church (Acts 14:23). Time and again, fasting is accompanied by prayer in the Bible.

While abstaining from food is one of the most common ways to fast, abstaining from behaviors or thoughts can be powerful too. Consciously choosing to not have the last word, or to stop arguing with a family member, or, even, to rid yourself of negative thoughts is a great way to practice the pillar of fasting. One year, I abstained from verbally correcting my husband. Crazy, I know. I openly admit to having an annoying habit—especially after I've had a rough day—of parenting him in the same way I do children. Not only does it drive him nuts, but it drives a wedge between us each time I do it. One night at dinner, as he bit his spoon after each spoonful of Ash Wednesday soup (a major no-no in my big book of table etiquette), I instead offered up quiet thanks that I was married to such a wonderful man who cares for, loves, and provides for our family. It's amazing how calming the peace was that settled on our family that Lent. The coupling of fasting and prayer is so powerful and is something our sisters and brothers in heaven practiced routinely. It's something we can learn to practice throughout the year too.

Here is one last thought on fasting. As we fast, we make space where there once was none. When Jesus fasted for forty days and forty nights, he created a lot of space. When Satan tempted him that day in the desert with an offer of bread, Jesus—through his fast—had created so much room for God that he quickly fought off the temptation and replied, "One does not live by bread alone, but by every word that comes from the mouth of God" (Matthew 4:4). He echoed the words of Deuteronomy 8:3, words spoken to the Israelites as part of their covenant with God. We, too, have this same source of sustenance ready for us to feast on. God's Word is always there, waiting to nourish our souls.

Almsgiving

Almsgiving is linked to our baptismal commitment; it's a way we care for others and express our gratitude for all that God has given us. Whenever I think of almsgiving, I think of one of my favorite childhood movies: *Robin Hood*. I've always had a soft spot for heroic men! In the film, Friar Tuck would ring his bell while crying out, "Alms! Alms for the poor!" as the townsfolk dropped coins into his basket.

Making a financial donation serves others not only during Lent but all year long. Most Americans are blessed to have a roof over their heads and a place to call home. For 100 million others worldwide, there is nothing but the street to live on. Another 1.6 billion live in tents and shacks.[16] We have so much compared to so many—so why is it that we often feel unhappy? When we take time to focus on those around who have less, we see how much goodness we have in our own lives. "If you lavish your food on the hungry and satisfy the afflicted; Then your light shall rise in darkness, and your gloom shall become like midday" (Isaiah 58:10).

My family and I prepare and serve dinner once a month at a local shelter. It never fails: No matter how long the workday was, no matter how much homework still needs to be completed, no matter how bad the traffic was on the drive over, we leave the shelter with thankful hearts. We're thankful for the gifts we have, grateful for each other, thankful for the opportunity to serve, and thankful to be reminded of God's love.

Home Traditions

The days leading up to Ash Wednesday are a lovely time to begin thinking about how you will pray, fast, and give, and about how each of those pillars will recenter and refocus you on the pathway to Christ. In my family, over a bowl of Ash Wednesday soup, we each fill out a Lenten promise card. This card gives us a chance to write down how each of us will grow in prayer, fasting, and almsgiving. Once completed, we keep our promise cards in a basket on the table and talk about them throughout Lent. Not only does writing our promises provide accountability and clarity on how we plan to journey through Lent, but it also proves to be an excellent record of how much we've grown! Sacrifices that even three years ago were a big deal have become part of our everyday lives. The first year we completed the cards, we each wrote that we would pray before meals. It was both hard and awkward at the start. Now, years later, it's a natural part of our suppertime routine.

Contemplate the Celebration

1. When we fast, we are asked to give up something that is, perhaps, taking up too much space in our lives. When we fast from it, we create room for God to move in and move us. What is something that is taking up too much space in your life right now?

_____

_____

_____

_____

_____

_____

_____

_____

_____

_____

2. Throughout the year, we are called to pray, fast, and give alms—
   especially during the season of Lent. Which of these three pillars is
   the easiest for you? Which is the most challenging? Why?

_____

_____

_____

_____

_____

_____

_____

_____

_____

3. Receiving ashes on Ash Wednesday is an opportunity for us to recognize our own mortality. If we leave our ashes on throughout the day, it also identifies us as Christians. How does being identified as a Christian by those you meet throughout the day make you feel? In addition to receiving ashes on Ash Wednesday, what are other ways you can "street evangelize" throughout the year?

4. Living Liturgically through Tradition: How does your family celebrate Lent? In what ways can you use your existing traditions to bring you closer to Christ?

_____

_____

_____

_____

_____

_____

_____

_____

_____

_____

Closing Prayer

Dear God, there are so many ways I can grow closer to you. In my prayer life, I want to remember more often that I can talk to you anytime. Through my actions of self-denial during Lent, I am offered a powerful glimpse of the sacrifice Christ made for me. In caring for others, I fulfill Jesus' command to do for others as he has done for us (John 13:15). Thank you for giving me three solid, fruitful pillars upon which to build a stronger foundation of faith.

Lent is a season to focus my life on penitential acts in preparation for the Resurrection celebration to come on Easter Sunday. Prayer, fasting, and almsgiving create an opportunity for me to recenter and refocus on the pathway to Christ.

This chapter has inspired me to consider all the magnificent ways I can bring more prayer into my life. Lord, continue to show me how I can make time for conversation with you to fortify our relationship. Lord, reveal where you want me to give. Help me not only to deliver from my surplus bravely, but also to dip into my poverty and share from my heart.

When I feel least like refraining from food, television, or any of the many worldly pleasures I enjoy, provide me with the strength to maintain my fast. Help me to discover what I gain during my fast rather than to focus on what I am giving up. Most importantly, let my fast make room for you in my schedule, my heart, and my life.

Invigorate my faith by the power of the Holy Spirit as I continue to reflect on the liturgical year, the Scriptures, and the questions to ponder. May each chapter in this study draw me closer and closer to you. Amen.

5: Holy Week, Triduum, and Easter

MAKE EVERY DAY BLESSED

Opening Prayer

Lord, each day, I want to remember your life, death, and resurrection with joy and gratitude. I want to remember the sacrifice you made for me out of your incomparable love. With all my imperfections, my doubts, my challenges, still you love me with a passion so remarkable that, even if I were the only person on earth, you still would have suffered all you did to save my soul.

I want to rejoice in your resurrection, in your victory over death. You have opened the gates of heaven for me, and my hope is in heaven, my true home! I am eternally grateful for all that you have done and will continue to do for me.

After forty days of penance and prayer during Lent, the anticipation of the special event about to take place begins to build. The last week of Lent begins on Palm Sunday and lasts through sunset on Holy Saturday. We are invited throughout Holy Week to stay and pray with you. Although I was not with you in the Garden of Gethsemane, I will keep watch for the three hours of your crucifixion. I will pray to not be so weary that I doze as the apostles did on that dreadful night. Please, Lord, I pray that I will not be caught sleepy and unaware.

Thank you, Lord, for your sacrificial love and the endless opportunities during Holy Week and Easter to grow in my faith. Thank you for unfathomable love that provides endless possibilities for growing in relationship with you. As I draw closer to you during the holiest season of the year, may I experience, in a very tangible way, your drawing ever closer to me. May every page of this study bring me one step nearer to you. Amen.

On My Heart

_____

_____

_____

_____

_____

_____

_____

_____

_____

_____

_____

_____

_____

Celebrating Holy Week, Triduum, and Easter

Palm Sunday, the last Sunday of Lent, is also the beginning of Holy Week. It's a time during which we commemorate and celebrate the final, culminating events of Jesus' earthly life. The period from Palm Sunday to Easter Sunday spans eight days, and my family and I find ourselves at our church for five of those eight days. For us, celebrating Holy Week and the Triduum are inextricably linked with time at our "home away from home"—our church and our parish community.

The traditions of Holy Week can be traced back to the legalization of Christianity in the early fourth century when early Christians would gather at various holy places throughout Jerusalem.[17] Through song, worship, and prayer, they would both commemorate and celebrate what took place at each location: Jesus' entry into Jerusalem; Judas's betraying him for thirty coins; the Last Supper in the upper room; the crucifixion; and the Resurrection. Isn't it beautiful to think that we, two thousand years later, are still commemorating and celebrating these events?

Palm Sunday

Holy Week begins on Palm Sunday, the day Jesus triumphantly entered Jerusalem on the back of a donkey. As he entered the city, palms were placed on the ground before him. As a Catholic community, we commemorate his entry into Jerusalem each year in our own way; members of the congregation receive palm fronds representing those that were placed before Christ so many years ago. During the Mass, these are held, blessed, and, in some churches, even waved, heralding Christ the King's entry into Jerusalem. If you live in an area of the world where it's hard to obtain palm fronds, you may receive branches from native trees such as box, olive, willow, or yew.

The palm fronds are blessed either before the start of Mass or during the Mass. Because the palms are blessed, they are sacramentals, objects that are set apart, blessed by the priest, and meant to draw us closer to the seven sacraments (*Catechism*, 1667).[18] They are not swords or spears, though many of the youngest parishioners have a knack for turning the fronds into weapons during Mass! Because the palm fronds are sacramentals, we take very special care of them in our home. My son learned to fold them into a cross, which he hangs above his door each year. On Palm Sunday, we also take down the previous year's palms and burn them in the backyard fire pit.[19]

At our parish, the 10:30 a.m. Mass is affectionately known as "the kids' Mass" because the church offers a children's liturgy at the same time. The children leave their families just before the Liturgy of the Word begins and return before the Liturgy of the Eucharist starts. At no Mass, though, is the children's liturgy more popular than on Palm Sunday! The children, palm swords—I mean, fronds—in hand, march off to hear the telling of the Passion of Our Lord.

Although some people grumble at having to stand for "such a long reading" or perhaps check out because they think, "I have heard this before," the reading of the Passion, especially on Palm Sunday, is a profound moment in Holy Week. We begin Palm Sunday Mass lauding Jesus as king, singing, The King of Glory comes and the nation rejoices," but all too quickly we turn on him, shouting, "Crucify him, crucify him!" While the children may be using their palms as swords, those of us re-enacting those poignant moments from two thousand years ago are using our words to pierce Jesus' heart once again.

Triduum and Easter Sunday

The Easter Triduum is the three days spanning Holy Thursday, Good Friday, and Holy Saturday. The start of the Triduum, with the Mass of the Lord's Supper on Holy Thursday, marks the end of Lent. There are Masses on Holy Thursday and Holy Saturday and services on Good Friday, and many of the faithful attend them all as part of their Lenten journey. Just like Ash Wednesday, these are not holy days of obligation.

On Holy Thursday, our family attends Mass; it begins with the recounting of the Last Supper and Jesus' betrayal by one of his own. Like Mass on Palm Sunday, there are several beautiful ways in which this celebration is different from others. First, during this Mass, the priest will wash the feet of the parishioners. This humble act mirrors the way Jesus washed the feet of his disciples so many years ago, making himself their servant.

There is also a unique way Holy Thursday Mass ends ... because it doesn't actually "end." As the celebration draws to a close, the Eucharist is carried forth by the priest with the congregation following behind him in procession. In our parish, we process singing, "Jesus, remember me when you come into your kingdom." It's a moment when time slows down, a moment in which I feel that I am speaking directly with Jesus, asking to be remembered.

The Eucharistic procession continues to the tabernacle, placed on a side or alternative altar, for distribution during the Good Friday service. The congregation is invited to stay before the tabernacle with Jesus and pray with him throughout the night. It was on this night so many years ago that Jesus retreated to the Garden of Gethsemane to pray. I think of the disciples often as my family and I spend a quiet time in adoration. Luke tells us that the disciples in the garden with Jesus were "sleeping from grief" when Jesus wakes them, telling them to "Get up and pray that you may not undergo the test" (Luke 22:46). I think of all those times in the past year that I've been tested and reflect on each test's outcome. This deep reflection time is often the pinnacle of my Lenten season.

After heading home for a decent night's sleep, we wake on the morning of Good Friday. It's a day of fasting to help keep our focus on Christ's Passion, crucifixion, and death. On Good Friday, there is no Mass, no consecration of the hosts; there is only a beautiful service that includes venerating the cross, a litany of prayers for the Church, and reception of Holy Communion.

There may be a Liturgy of the Word, but there is no Liturgy of the Eucharist—the reserved consecrated hosts from Holy Thursday are distributed during the Good Friday service. As we walk into the service in silence, a bare altar stands before us and the absence of any song conveys the solemnity of this day. The door of the tabernacle sits open, and the tabernacle itself is empty. We experience a sense of loss in the death of Our Lord. The entire focus of this liturgy is on the cross at Calvary. Some parishes—like ours—will have a veneration of the cross. We adore not the cross itself but what it represents: our sinfulness and Jesus' willingness to die on it. The service ends with parishioners exiting the church in complete silence.

On Good Friday, we also attend Stations of the Cross when we can. Usually, at either noon or 3:00 p.m. (the hour of Jesus' death), we journey with Jesus to the cross before we celebrate his glorious resurrection during the Easter Vigil. One year, we hope to attend a local prayer service called the Three Hours, which occurs between noon and 3:00 p.m.—the hours of Jesus' suffering on the cross. Our parish also holds a Passion play, or a reenactment of Christ's last days.

The Easter Vigil is celebrated late Saturday evening. It is as though we are holding a vigil outside the tomb. Perhaps one of the most beautiful Masses of the year, the evening starts in silence outside the church, with the lighting of the new Paschal candle and each parishioner (often) receiving a small candle lit from the Paschal candle as they process as a group into the dark church. My heart sings at this Mass; never have I felt such beauty or anticipation as when we all stand together in darkness, holding our small white candles. I feel a bit like the children of Israel, who were guided at night by a pillar of fire—we, as Christians, now follow the risen Christ. Once inside the church, the individual candles are blown out, and either the deacon or priest reads the Easter Proclamation. Sometimes sung, this great poetic text proclaims of the mystery of our salvation![20] Then salvation history is recounted through the reading of nine Scripture passages: seven from the Old Testament and two from the New Testament. Before the Gospel is proclaimed, the congregation sings a glorious alleluia. At our church, the entrance, chant, and readings usually take about an hour or so—at which point our priest jokingly starts his homily by saying, "We've only just begun!"

What he says is true, though—we've only just begun this wonderful celebration. Next, candidates undergoing the Rite of Christian Initiation for Adults (RCIA) receive the sacraments of Baptism and Confirmation. We, too, renew our baptismal promises. Afterward, we celebrate the Liturgy of the Eucharist.

Easter Sunday Mass celebrates the Resurrection in its entirety! The structure of Easter Sunday Mass, though joyous in the decor, song, and praise, is very similar to other weekend Masses. The atmosphere is vibrant; good has triumphed over evil, and Our Lord has risen!

The Easter season—a fifty-day celebration ending at Pentecost—begins with the celebration at the Easter Vigil Mass. The fifty days of Easter outshine the somber days of Lent, for, indeed, we have something to celebrate! Easter is the most important celebration for Christians, even more important than Christmas. Each of us was born to a father and mother, just as Jesus was. None of us, in the fulfillment of Old Testament prophecy, died and rose from the dead to give eternal life to those willing to accept God's gift. It is the Resurrection that is at the heart of our faith, and the celebrations of Easter—and preparations leading up to it—become more relevant (and reverent) in this light.

Visible Signs That Holy Week, Triduum, and Easter Are Here

Last summer, my son attended what he affectionately calls "Rosary camp." During this inspiring five-day camp, children spent their days learning the mysteries of the Rosary under the guidance of seminarians and Dominican sisters. His most significant takeaway, though, was the desire to create a small prayer space in our home, which we readily agreed to.

Throughout the year, we update this special space to reflect the changing liturgical seasons. When Lent begins, we keep this space almost barren. On Good Friday, we cover the area in a black cloth to represent the death of Jesus. This cloth remains in place through Sunday, when we replace it with a white cloth, dyed eggs, and just about every other Easter decoration we have, to celebrate the Resurrection. This simple decor in our home creates a purposeful space for us. Decorating it during Holy Week and the triduum makes the celebration of the Resurrection even more powerful. We've finished our fast, and we relish in the feast of Our Lord!

Invitation to Ponder

At the Easter Vigil and at Easter Sunday Mass, we renew our baptismal vows. As a congregation, we respond "yes" to questions such as, "Do you reject sin, so as to live in the freedom of God's children?" "Do you reject the glamour of evil?" and "Do you believe in the Holy Spirit, the holy catholic Church, the communion of saints, the forgiveness of sins, the resurrection of the body, and the life everlasting?"

Sometimes, as we respond "yes" as a group, I find myself wanting to say "mostly." I reject sin, but there *was* this one time I willingly held a grudge against a friend. I reject the glamour of evil, but I *do* spend a small fortune on designer blue jeans. It's not something I'm proud of, but it's the truth. If you were asked to renew your baptismal promises today, how would you answer the questions above? Do you have a few "mostly" responses too?

_____

_____

_____

_____

_____

_____

_____

_____

_____

_____

_____

_____

_____

_____

_____

_____

_____

_____

_____

_____

_____

_____

Connecting to Scripture

PRAYER TO THE HOLY SPIRIT BEFORE READING SCRIPTURE

Come, Holy Spirit. Fill me with every grace and blessing necessary to understand the message, prepared for and awaiting me, in the Scriptures. May I grow deeper in faith, in hope, and in love with Jesus as I spend this time with the Word of God. Amen.

Isaiah 40:31 _____

_____

_____

🕊 Matthew 6:1 _____

_____

_____

🕊 Matthew 21:1-11 _____

_____

_____

🕊 Matthew 26:47 _____

_____

_____

🕊 Matthew 28:1-15 _____

_____

_____

Scripture Reflection

The beauty of Holy Week is that we, two thousand years later, can actively participate in events that took place during Jesus' final days. We've talked at length about how we, as Catholics, remember the last week of Jesus' life here on Earth. Now let's talk about how our celebrations at church and at home reflect the events that took place during that week. For me, each day is an opportunity to reflect on different aspects of my life and actions.

Welcoming Our King

Jesus entered Jerusalem riding on the back of a donkey in fulfillment of the Old Testament prophecy. While the small donkey may not have been the golden chariot that we often associate with grand kingly entrances, Jesus was received into the city as a king: "The very large crowd spread their cloaks on the road, while others cut branches from the trees and strewed them on the road. The crowds preceding him and those following kept crying out and saying: 'Hosanna to the Son of David; blessed is he who comes in the name of the Lord; hosanna in the highest'" (Matthew 21:8–9). The crowds not only welcomed him as blessed but also recognized him as the Son of David: the one who would lead them to the Promised Land.

We love displaying the palms in our home, folded in half and placed behind the wooden crucifix my husband made. They are a reminder of our willingness to follow Jesus and to welcome him into our city and home. They're a reminder, too, for those days when I'm feeling a bit less like welcoming Jesus into the city—those days when I don't want to wake up early for Mass after a late Saturday night, or those evenings when I read an extra chapter before bed instead of taking time to pray. Then, I walk by the palms. I remember the reception Jesus received from the crowds when he entered the city. I recall the way these same people turned on him so quickly just five days later. In those moments, I feel like that fickle crowd, and I refocus myself so I can find renewed strength to welcome my Lord.

Chubby Little Feet

On the morning of what we now celebrate as Holy Thursday, Jesus commissioned Peter and John to go into the city and prepare a space so that they could celebrate the Passover meal. This meal is commemorated in our faith traditions as the start of the triduum. There are so many beautiful stories in Scripture about the Last Supper, but I especially love the story of Jesus washing the disciples' feet. Practically, it was a necessary action—the sandaled feet of the disciples would surely have been dusty and dirty from the day's long walks. There is a deeper meaning here though. Jesus washed his disciples' feet not only to clean them but also to teach them a lesson in humility: He, their teacher, their Savior, is not above loving and caring for them. He gives of himself in this lesson to his disciples and expects them to do the same once he is gone.

My young son has experienced the gift of having his feet washed twice—and he is only six years old! The first time, he was the cutest seven-month-old infant. He cooed as the cool water was poured over his chubby little feet, captivated by what our priest was doing. The moment was one belonging to him and Father Mike, just the two of them. The second time was this past year, and, as a six-year-old, it was quite a different experience for him. My son understood the grand meaning behind the ritual but was much more interested in having his friends see him in front of the church. I can excuse him for that because of his age, but the experience left me feeling unsettled.

I thought about the times in my life when I was more concerned with the way I appeared to others than what was taking place before me: presenting the perfect Easter brunch, giving the best gifts at Christmas, or showing the most pious face at confession (seriously, I've done that). It's in those moments that Matthew 6:1 comes to mind: "Take care not to perform righteous deeds so that people may see them; otherwise, you will have no recompense from your heavenly Father." I recognize that I've let the outside world, again, take hold of what is essential. Instead of being discouraged, I choose to refocus.

Humility and Loss

When he was younger, my son and I walked to our local farmers market almost every week. He would buy a honey stick from the beekeeper, we would share pancit noodles from Mr. Ed on the steps of St. Mary's, and then we would enter the chapel for a few moments of adoration. While adoration with a child isn't an hour-long affair (more like four minutes), I found myself often meditating on what Jesus went through in his final days. The humiliation and mockery he endured, moment after moment, would break even the strongest; it would surely break me.

Saint Faustina wrote extensively on humility: "Humiliation is my daily food. I understand that the bride must herself share in everything that is the groom's; and so, His cloak of mockery must cover me, too. At those times when I suffer much, I try to remain silent, as I do not trust my tongue which, at such moments, is inclined to talk for itself, while its duty is to help me praise God for all the blessings and gifts which He has given me."[21] She, like Jesus, understood the power of suffering—an understanding we can layer over our own lives as well.

Jesus provides us the most beautiful example of humble obedience and surrender to the will of God during great suffering. After celebrating his last meal with his disciples, Jesus goes to the Garden of Gethsemane to pray and is arrested there in the early hours of the morning. He is tried before the crowd, crucified at noon, and dies at 3 p.m. A wealthy landowner and believer in Jesus, Joseph of Arimathea, provides his tomb for Jesus' body. Jesus is laid to rest in the late afternoon, before the start of the Sabbath at sundown.

When Christ was crucified, everything he had—everything—was taken from him. John 19:23–24 describes that lots were cast for his garments. Just as each of our lives is a gift, so, too, are the tangible things in it. It is as though everything we have is on loan from the Father and can be taken or given away at any time.

Living as we do in southern California, wildfires are a part of our life. We've been evacuated multiple times over the past few years and are thankful that our home has never sustained damage. Others have not been as fortunate. The response from families in the face of such tragedy has been so beautiful. While those families experienced such devastation, they were thankful that the loss was in material goods only. Their gratitude reminds me of Jesus; just as Jesus' earthly life ended, he was grateful for the love of his Father and bowed to God's will. We, too, can thank God with a grateful heart for everything, even when it is all taken from us.

The Waiting Game

Holy Saturday is a day of waiting—a day of great anticipation. There is little in Scripture about what took place on Holy Saturday, but it is easy to imagine the waiting of the disciples, the waiting of Mary, the waiting of believers throughout Jerusalem and neighboring cities. They knew something special was to come, something that would change their lives forever: "They that hope in the Lord will renew their strength, they will soar on eagles' wings; They will run and not grow weary, walk and not grow faint" (Isaiah 40:31). The strength that the disciples had well before the Holy Spirit touched them on Pentecost was limitless. The man they had given up everything to follow had been killed. They waited. They were strengthened, and they ran to the tomb the next day.

I know about waiting, although it is not an area in which I excel. My husband was not Catholic when we started dating at age eighteen, nor was he Catholic when we married at the age twenty-five. It was a good friend of his who often accompanied me to Mass while we were still in college. After we were married, my husband would occasionally join me for Mass—but only on weeks when he needed something from Home Depot, which was right next to the church. He was ok with my faith and agreed that we would raise our children in the Catholic Church, but he never made any mention of his conversion. It was something I prayed for, but it was also something that I knew would only happen in God's time   if at all. It was a question-filled wait. What if he changed his mind about raising our family in the Catholic faith? What if he began to resent the role it played in my life? What if he never heard God's call in his heart? Just like Jesus' followers on that Holy Saturday so long ago, I waited. I waited, praying at the altar, asking for Saint Monica's intercessions—and now I continue to offer prayers of thanks because, just before his thirtieth birthday, he was baptized into the faith.

The Feminine Genius

Sometimes, I wonder if God has a soft spot in his heart for women. One of my favorite Scripture stories is that of Mary Magdalene on Easter Sunday. It was early that Sunday morning, before sunrise. To whom did Jesus appear? Two women. "Jesus met them on their way and greeted them. They approached, embraced his feet, and did him homage" (Matthew 28:9). After their encounter with the risen Lord, they rushed back to the disciples in the upper room to share news of Christ's resurrection.

As a woman, this story has an extra special meaning to me. When we think back to Jesus' death on the cross, we know that it was a woman to whom he spoke some of his last words, when he told his mother, Mary, that he was entrusting her care to his beloved disciple. A short time later, it was two women to whom he spoke his first words after his resurrection. God's love for all his children—men and women— pours out on Easter Sunday!

Contemplate the Celebration

1. What kind of welcome did Jesus receive as he entered Jerusalem, a city under the leadership of Rome? (The story is found in Matthew 21:1–11.) Think, now, about what the procession would have looked like had it been the Roman king, Tiberius Caesar, entering the city. What similarities and differences would there have been? What kind of a king do we serve today?

_____

_____

_____

_____

_____

_____

_____

_____

_____

_____

2. God does not abandon us when we suffer, but, instead, he uses that suffering as an opportunity to draw us closer to him. What humiliations and sufferings have you experienced in your life? How can you use those experiences to, as Saint Faustina writes, "praise God for all the blessings and gifts which he has given" to you?[22]

_____

_____

_____

_____

_____

_____

_____

_____

_____

_____

3. Pope Saint John Paul II wrote about the "genius of women" and their importance in the life of the Church. What role do you play in your church community? What gifts do you have that you can share?[23]

_____

_____

_____

_____

_____

_____

_____

_____

_____

_____

_____

4. Living Liturgically through Tradition: How does your family celebrate the Triduum and Easter? In what ways can you use your
   existing traditions to bring you closer to Christ?

_____

_____

_____

_____

_____

_____

_____

_____

_____

_____

_____

_____

Closing Prayer

Dear God, thank you for sending your Son to model acceptance of your great love for me. Thank you for sending the Holy Spirit to accompany me on my earthly journey. The days can be long and hard, yet I live with the hope of salvation deep within my soul.

Easter Sunday Mass celebrates the Resurrection in its entirety! The joy does, indeed, come in the morning. Thank you, Lord, for the promise of the dawn after every darkness. I rejoice at the thought of the glorious dawn of your bursting from the tomb and the opening of heaven's gates. Lord, always remain with me on my earthly journey, that I may one day experience the ultimate joy of an eternal Easter with you.

Invigorate my faith by the power of the Holy Spirit as I continue to reflect on the liturgical year, the Scriptures, and the questions to ponder. May each chapter draw me closer and closer to you. Amen.

6: Ordinary Time

Opening Prayer

Heavenly Father, ignite within my heart the desire to seek occasions to celebrate you throughout the year. Help me through this chapter to embrace the beauty and spiritual blessings of Ordinary Time. During Ordinary Time, the readings at Mass focus on Jesus' teachings and his life with the disciples. In the other liturgical seasons, we learn of Jesus' sacrificial life for the love of us. After rejoicing at his birth and marveling at his Passion, we now seek to walk with him in everything, every day.

Glorious Father, I long to appreciate Ordinary Time as much as the other seasons, especially because I am called to celebrate and rejoice throughout the year! Let me be a woman who lives Philippians 4:4, which says, "Rejoice in the Lord always. I shall say it again: rejoice!" Inspire within me a deep desire to celebrate with you every single day.

Thank you for your unchanging love and the daily opportunities to grow in my faith. Thank you for unfathomable love that provides ordinary, everyday moments to grow in relationship with you. As I draw closer to you, I am coming to see and believe that you draw ever closer to me. May every page of this study bring me one step nearer to you. Amen.

On My Heart

_____

_____

_____

_____

_____

_____

_____

_____

_____

_____

_____

_____

_____

_____

_____

_____

_____

_____

Celebrating the Season of Ordinary Time

When I was in college, one of the top songs we heard at my (now) husband's fraternity parties was Coolio's "1-2-3-4," which included the line, "Ain't no party like a west coast party 'cause a west coast party don't stop!" The song, while not politically (or grammatically) correct, is a lot like our faith: Ain't no party like a Catholic party 'cause a Catholic party don't stop! Being Catholic means we are celebrating the richness of our faith all year long. Our faith is not limited to just Advent, Christmas, Lent, and Easter. We celebrate feast days, saint days, and even changes of the season during Ordinary Time.

The liturgical seasons in which we celebrate the birth, death, and resurrection of Our Lord and Savior can be hectic. So much energy is dedicated to these major feasts that we need some down time—some ordinary time—to breathe. I take liberties with the word here, though, for *ordinary* doesn't refer to commonplace days or days without significance. Ordinary time gets its name because its weeks are ordinal (numbered in order); you'll often hear the weeks talked about as "the tenth week in Ordinary Time" or "the twentieth week in Ordinary Time."

During Ordinary Time, the readings at Mass focus on Jesus' teachings and his life with the disciples. Just as we walked with Jesus through his birth, death, and resurrection, we again walk with him during his everyday life.[24]

Do you go to daily Mass? I go occasionally, but it's not something that's part of my everyday routine. There is a group of older women at our parish, though, who meets each morning for 8:00 Mass and then gather on the plaza for a cup of coffee. They've been doing it for years and have created a beautiful support network for one another.

In a way, they remind me of a living version of the daily Mass they just left: just as we walked with Christ through the readings, they walk beside each other. So beautiful.

Twice the Fun

One of my very good friends is the mother of twins. She often jokes that it's twice the fun—usually right after changing double dirty diapers! Like her beautiful twins, Ordinary Time is twice the fun because we experience this season twice a year.

The first season of Ordinary Time begins the day after the Baptism of the Lord in January and continues through the Tuesday before Ash Wednesday, commonly referred to as Fat Tuesday, Shrove Tuesday, or, even, Pancake Tuesday. Pancake Tuesday is a favorite in our home; each year my husband fries up a batch of crispy bacon alongside a steaming stack of pancakes and a side of scrambled eggs. I prepare a delicious apple compote. The apples, cinnamon, honey, and splash of bourbon simmer all day in the Crock-Pot and make such a delicious topping for our pancakes!

The second season of Ordinary Time begins on the Monday following Pentecost and continues through the Saturday before Advent. Combined, these two periods of Ordinary Time are longer than any other liturgical season. We celebrate Ordinary Time for either thirty-three or thirty-four weeks per year, depending on when key dates like Christmas and Easter fall.

You may have heard the weeks between major liturgical seasons referred to as "the Sundays after Epiphany" or "the Sundays after Pentecost." That's because the introduction of Ordinary Time—numbering each of the thirty-tree (or thirty-four) weeks—is a newer tradition that came about after the Second Vatican Council.[25] On the occasions when we go to a parish that still celebrates the Latin Mass, the traditional terms are used.

Holy Days of Obligation

While celebrating Mass during the Saturday vigil or on Sunday is our obligation as Catholics, there are also other days when we are required to attend the Eucharistic celebration. These are known as holy days of obligation.

I'm a list girl, so, if you're like me, here's a nice tidy list of holy days of obligation here in the United States, including the days that fall outside of Ordinary Time. It's important to note that some of these may vary by country, as countries often have feast days that are important to their history. For example, Saint Patrick's Day is a holy day of obligation in Ireland, just as the feast day of Our Lady of Guadalupe is in Mexico.

- **January 1:** Solemnity of Mary, the Holy Mother of God

- **Thursday of the Sixth Week of Easter:** Solemnity of the Ascension of the Lord (observed on the following Sunday in most dioceses of the United States)

- **August 15:** Solemnity of the Assumption of the Blessed Virgin Mary

- **November 1:** Solemnity of All Saints

- **December 8:** Solemnity of the Immaculate Conception of the Blessed Virgin Mary

⤷ **December 25:** Solemnity of the Nativity of Our Lord
Jesus Christ

In our family, we have our own "obligation days." These days are obligatory only to us but are days we wouldn't miss! Each year, we celebrate our name days (feast days honoring the saints whose names we share) and our baptismal anniversaries. I love celebrating the anniversaries of our baptisms; we bake angel food cake with fresh strawberries and pull out photos from our baptismal days. It's such a simple yet meaningful way for us to commemorate that important day!

Rogation and Ember Days

We couldn't talk about the liturgical year without bringing up Rogation and Ember Days. These days of petition and thanksgiving—while they do not constitute a separate liturgical season—have been a part of our Church's history for more than 1,500 years.

Rogation and Ember days were removed from the liturgical calendar following the reforms of the Second Vatican Council; today, it's up to the local bishops' conference in each country to determine whether and how to celebrate these days.[26] That said, individuals are free to celebrate the days on their own—and some still do.

Rogation days are the days we observe at the change of season. These are days for people to come together in prayer to ask God to bless fields, harvests, and even a parish. One of my good friends has the most beautiful garden in her backyard. Her garden is surrounded by fruit trees and has a chicken coop at its center; she often refers to her garden as her opportunity to be an urban farmer. Last year, we celebrated the Major Rogation (April 25) at her house, where we had our farm-to-table meal. In addition to the Major Rogation, there are three Minor Rogations which are celebrated on the Monday, Tuesday, and Wednesday immediately before Ascension Thursday (forty days after Easter).

Ember days, more numerous than Rogation days, also mark the changing of the seasons. In the spring, we celebrate spring Ember days on the Wednesday, Friday, and Saturday after the first Sunday of Lent; summer Ember days fall on the Wednesday, Friday, and Saturday after Pentecost; fall Ember days occur on the Wednesday, Friday, and Saturday after the third Sunday in September; and the winter Ember days are the Wednesday, Friday, and Saturday after the Feast of Saint Lucy (December 13). While the calendaring of Ember days may seem cumbersome, they are intended to remind us that all we have comes from God and should be placed under his loving care.

Getting to Know One Another

After the hustle and bustle of the busier liturgical seasons, Ordinary Time can be a welcome season of rest. I always experience powerful, faith-affirming feelings around Easter and Christmas. Yet, to me, these "bursts of faith" are fleeting and fade over time. It wasn't until I started being more purposeful with my spiritual life during Ordinary Time that my faith really took hold. Sister Joan Chittister, O.S.B., a Benedictine nun, once said, "A bit at a time, we begin to feel the great magnet of the liturgical year draw us more and more into the one clear message: in the liturgical year we live the life of Jesus day after day until finally one day it becomes our own. ... We ourselves become players in the great drama of bringing the reign of God to the turmoil of the world."[27]

During this season of the liturgical calendar, we can get to know Mary better. We can learn from the saints, our heavenly brothers and sisters who are always available to intercede for us. We experience the entirety of the Gospel at Mass. The breadth of our faith can be taken in during Ordinary Time, allowing the threads of our faith to take hold and weave a cloak that we find shelter under all year long.

Visible Signs That Ordinary Time Is Here

When you walk into some people's homes, you know you are walking into a home filled with faith. My grandparents had the image of Divine Mercy on their living room wall and a painting of the Last Supper above their kitchen table. A close friend has an image of Our Lady of Guadalupe hanging above her piano and a wall-mounted holy water font beside her front door.

Does this mean you need statues throughout your house to have a proper Catholic home? Absolutely not! We are each uniquely made, and the ways in which we turn our houses into homes are different for each of us.

God created humans with five senses. Each of these senses offers an opportunity for us to experience our Catholic faith. I am a visual person at heart, so the sight of beautiful Scripture quotes on the walls of our home provides me with grounding moments throughout the day. My husband is a foodie, so we incorporate many delicious baked goods, ice cream sundaes, and main dishes to commemorate feast days. What's most important is that you do you. We are meant to be inspired by one another, not feel pressured to do exactly what another person is doing. Take some quiet time in prayer to figure out simple ways that you can incorporate your faith into the environment around you, and you'll create a space that is all your own.

Invitation to Ponder

It is easier to "be Catholic" during the more focused liturgical seasons of Lent, Easter, Advent, and Christmas. But we spend most of our days of the year in Ordinary Time, and it is during this time that we have the chance to grow in faith consistently. Whether it be through regular attendance at weekend Mass, participating in Bible studies, joining a ministry, or leading a prayer group, the options to grow abound. What does your faith life look like during these thirty-three weeks?

Connecting to Scripture

PRAYER TO THE HOLY SPIRIT BEFORE READING SCRIPTURE

Come, Holy Spirit. Fill me with every grace and blessing necessary to understand the message, prepared for and awaiting me, in the Scriptures. May I grow deeper in faith, in hope, and in love with Jesus as I spend this time with the Word of God. Amen.

⌁ Psalm 118:24 _____

_____

_____

⌁ Matthew 21:18–22 _____

_____

_____

⌁ Matthew 26:69–75 _____

_____

_____

⌁ Matthew 4:19 _____

_____

_____

𝄢 Philippians 4:4–5 _____

_____

_____

Scripture Reflection

"It's not easy being green," Kermit the Frog once said. When I notice the green vestments of Ordinary Time at Mass after a season of celebration, I sometimes agree! It feels a bit like the day after vacation has ended.

But over time, I've grown to appreciate Ordinary Time as much as the other seasons. After all, we are called to celebrate and rejoice throughout the year! Philippians 4:4 tells us, "Rejoice in the Lord always. I shall say it again: rejoice!" Not just sometimes, or only during Christmas and Easter, but always rejoice.

We are created by love and for love, and Our Creator doesn't want us to limit our celebration of that love to certain days of the year. All day, every day, God loves us. God leaves little gifts for us throughout the day: a smile here, a break in traffic there, a kind word from a stranger when it's most needed. If we were to slow down to recognize them, how different would our days, weeks, and lives be?

In Psalm 118:24, we read, "This is the day the LORD has made; let us rejoice in it and be glad." Every day is a gift. My life holds many reminders of this truth. My father had a routine physical one day, and the next he was diagnosed with cancer. My husband and I went out with a close friend one night, and the next day she called to say her husband had just walked out on her. We never know what tomorrow holds. Tomorrow may be the best day, or it may be the worst. All we know—all we have—is today. Let us rejoice and be glad!

Walking the Walk

While it may be a little easier to remember Christ on Christmas morning or on Easter Sunday, it is the days in between, I believe, that define us as Christians. One of my favorite Scripture readings starts in the early hours of a new day. Jesus' morning begins like many of ours: he wakes and is hungry. On his way into the city, he sees a fig tree; finding no fruit on it, he curses the tree. The disciples are amazed as the tree withers right before their eyes. A friend of mine joked that Jesus cursed the tree because he was "hangry" (you know, that hunger that makes us angry), but the message here is so much more.

Matthew 21:19 mentions the tree having leaves. Usually, we expect to find fruit hidden in the leaves of a healthy-looking fruit tree. In the case of this fig tree, there was none. Outwardly, the tree looked like it should have been fruitful. Inside, it was barren. With one of his final miracles, Jesus reminds his disciples (and us) of the hypocrisy of living a life that outwardly projects one image while our interior reality is completely different.

This point resonated for me when I realized my vocabulary changed depending on the company I kept. Around my Christian friends, it was easy to say things like, "I'll pray for you," or "It was such a blessing." Around my non-Christian friends, I replaced these common phrases with, "I hope it works out," and "I was so lucky." I was, like Peter in Matthew 26, choosing to distance myself from my faith around nonbelievers. While I never denied Jesus as directly as Peter did, I was doing so quietly with the changes in my words and actions. I wasn't living authentically and was, therefore, projecting an outward image that was different from what I felt inside, just as the fig tree was doing. Ouch.

Ordinary Time is a time to truly walk the walk of a Christian. It's a time when we have a chance to live our faith outside the significant celebratory days and be, each day, the person Our God created us to be.

Home Traditions

We love a good celebration with friends and enjoy just about any excuse to get together. With more than ten thousand saints and so many beautiful feast days, Ordinary Time is extraordinary! Some of our favorite traditions revolve around key celebrations during this season. I am of Eastern European descent, and every Shrove Tuesday we bake paczkis alongside our pancakes—sweet treats that use up the sugar and eggs that, in times past, were abstained from during the upcoming Lent. These baked Polish doughnuts, filled with sweetened fruits and rolled in powdered sugar, are the way we wrap up Ordinary Time. Yum! I'm salivating just thinking about them.

When we bake, the whole family gets involved. By the end, the kitchen is an explosion of yeast, flour, and sugar, mixed with the most amazing smells. Once baked, we put on our jackets and head out to deliver warm paczkis to all our neighbors, who have come to appreciate and anticipate the day as much as we have.

While that celebratory feast takes a lot of work, most of our other celebrations are simple. On January 8, we stop by Popeyes (that's "Pope-Yes" in our house, not "Pop-Eyes"!) for some Louisiana chicken, and share the story of Our Lady of Succor over Cajun beans and rice. On May 15, we plant tomatoes in honor of Saint Isidore the Farmer. Then on May 30, we watch the movie *Joan of Arc* in celebration of this heroic young saint. On November 1, we have an All Saints' Day costume party. We (try to) go to confession each month as a family, stopping for ice cream on the way home. ... Such simple acts, yet each an opportunity for renewal and growth.

Each of these small celebrations provides me with the opportunity to live authentically and grow in faith with my family and friends alongside me. Taking the paczkis to our neighbors gives us the chance to be lay witnesses on the street. Take a moment to reread Matthew 4:19 in your Bible. What does it mean to you to be a fisher of men? For me, it means living my faith openly with those both inside and outside of my Catholic community. It becomes a part of who I am and naturally flows out through all I do. By being a witness and sharing in an open, nonthreatening way, we can reach others and plant seeds as we strive to grow in holiness too.

Contemplate the Celebration

1. Ordinary Time can be so ... ordinary. Yet it's during our ordinary human experiences that the Spirit is most at work. Think of a time when you felt God's nearness, his hand guiding your heart. How can you use the quiet of Ordinary Time to create an openness and receptiveness to continually experience his guidance?

_____

_____

_____

_____

_____

_____

_____

_____

_____

_____

2. Jesus cursed the fig tree because it gave off the appearance of being full of figs when there were none. Sometimes, we can be like that fig tree. Does who you are on the inside match up with the image you project on the outside?

_____

_____

_____

_____

_____

_____

_____

_____

_____

_____

_____

_____

3. At the end of the Mass, we are told to "Go in peace," "Go forth pro-claiming Christ with your life," or "Go announce the Gospel with your life." In each of these dismissals, we are given a mission. We are told to "go." How can you personally go out into the world, sharing your faith with those around you? How have you been called to be a fisher of men?

_____

_____

_____

_____

_____

_____

_____

_____

_____

4. Living Liturgically through Tradition: How does your family cele-brate Ordinary Time? In what ways can you use your existing tradi-tions to bring you closer to Christ?

_____

_____

_____

_____

_____

_____

_____

_____

Closing Prayer

Jesus, each day is an opportunity for us to start over—to start anew. Thank you for the endless possibilities to grow in love, faith, and hope throughout the year.

During this time of the liturgical calendar, I want to get to know Mary, our model of faith. What a privilege and joy that the Lord has given each of us to learn from the saints, our heavenly brothers and sisters. What a privilege and joy to know they are always available as intercessors. Help me to turn daily to Mary and the communion of saints for assistance in my faith journey.

During this time in the liturgical calendar, remind me to not neglect my time in the Scriptures, especially the daily Mass readings. In her wisdom, the Church provides us with the entire Gospel and its wellspring of knowledge at Mass—a remarkable blessing to allow us to know Our Lord in a more intimate way.

Each of these small celebrations offered throughout Ordinary Time provides me with opportunity after opportunity to live authentically and grow in faith, with my family and friends alongside me.

Invigorate my faith by the power of the Holy Spirit as I continue to reflect on the liturgical year, the Scriptures, and the questions to ponder. May each chapter draw me closer and closer to you. Amen.

7: Living Liturgically

Opening Prayer

Lord, I need your help to dispel an ugly lie that has infiltrated too many of my thoughts. Lord, help me to realize that I do not need to live my Catholic faith or any aspect of my life perfectly. That lie sets me up to feel defeated, overwhelmed, and inadequate, none of which comes from you. Like any good parent, you ask only for my love and that I offer you my best effort.

Original sin plants a seed of doubt in our hearts. However, I am a beloved daughter of God, and, regardless of my skills in crafting, baking, planning, or any other activity, I am loved—loved with an everlasting, ever-merciful, and ever-perfect love.

Remind me, precious Lord, that life is about balance. As women, we are called to be and do so much with our feminine genius. We each have different gifts, different talents, and different lives that we are continually working to find balance in, while using those gifts for our world and the glory of God. Remind me of the abundant graces you bestow to assist me in recognizing my gifts and in achieving balance.

Thank you for your steadfast love and endless patience with me as I grow in my faith. Thank you for your perfect, unconditional love, which provides endless opportunities to deepen my relationship with you. As I draw closer to you by offering the gifts and talents you have blessed me with, I believe you have drawn ever closer to me. May every page in this study bring me one step nearer to you. Amen.

On My Heart

_____

_____

_____

_____

_____

_____

_____

_____

_____

_____

_____

_____

_____

_____

_____

_____

Celebrating All Year Long

My family has created many traditions as we have celebrated holidays and special occasions throughout the year. My mom always had something special for us to commemorate her favorite feast days—green milk on Saint Patrick's Day, coins in our shoes for Saint Nicholas Day, and sweet notes in our lunch box on Saint Valentine's Day.

Also, we would continue whatever celebration took place at school at our home. I remember having a May crowning of the Blessed Mother with my third-grade class and then coming home to make a flower wreath from the clovers in our yard to crown the statue of Mary my mom kept in her bedroom. For me, this seamless continuation of faith from school to family life to Mass on Sunday wove Catholicism into my very being. It's a part of who I am and is the lens through which I view the world around me, speak with others, and mark the passing of time.

"But I can't celebrate all year! We're already too busy with baseball games every weekend and piano practice at night. I don't even have food coloring to turn the milk green!" One of my favorite Scripture verses comes from 1 Corinthians 12:4–6: "There are different kinds of spiritual gifts but the same Spirit; there are different forms of service but the same Lord; there are different workings but the same God who produces all of them in everyone."

Now, I am not the best baker. I'm also not the butcher or the candlestick maker—but I can sew. I use this talent to sew table runners in liturgical colors for our home, Jesse Tree ornaments for Advent, and gorgeous snuggly quilts that we cuddle beneath. It's this passion that led me to start my business, Faith and Fabric, where I create faith-inspired quilt patterns and design Catholic fabrics for other sewists to use in their sewing projects. Sewing may not be your thing, but something else is.

Maybe you enjoy cooking, so your feast day celebrations could include whipping up a Mexican fiesta on December 12 in honor of Our Lady of Guadalupe or an Italian pasta bake for the feast of Saint Catherine of Siena on April 29. Perhaps you're a fashionista, in which case you may wish to choose outfits according to the feast day or the liturgical colors. If home decor is your passion, you might create beautiful prayer spaces and table displays centered on the liturgical seasons.

There seems to be a common misconception that we need to complete all tasks perfectly or not at all. That simply is not true; part of the fun of learning something new is trying it out and making it your own! Remember, you are a beloved daughter of God, and regardless of your crafting, baking, planning, or any other ability, you are loved. Think about your reaction when your son or daughter drew his or her first picture. Did you crinkle it up and throw it into the trash? Or, did you proudly place it front and center on your refrigerator?

Finding Balance and Staying Focused

Remember, it's about balance. It's something I continuously work to achieve; I'll bet you do too. As women, we are called to be and do so much with our feminine genius. For me, my "genius" has more than once left me empty and numb. You see, I'm guilty of being a "yes" person. Need help working the table before 8:30 a.m. Mass? Sure, I can do that. Can I stay to play with the music ministry at 10:30 a.m. Mass? No problem. Grab some photos of the families for the new directory this weekend? You got it. Suddenly, my cup is full—so full that it's spilling over the sides and puddling on the floor ... and it's only noon on a Sunday!

For me, prayer life suffers as a result of my overcommitment. My friend's prayer life leaves me in awe: she frequently attends morning Mass after dropping her children off at school and before heading to work, makes time to lead her family through the Rosary several times a week, and attends pro-life prayer vigils when she can. She's a saint in the making to me. Her prayer life and mine aren't comparable; her spiritual works and mine aren't equivalent—and they aren't meant to be.

We each have different gifts, different talents, and different lives in which we are continually working to find balance. My friend and I sometimes compare our differences, but we do it as a way of honoring them and sharing in the joys particular to our current vocations. Our lives, our families, and our upbringings are different as well. These differences manifest themselves in the ways we honor our faith using our own gifts. Unwrapping those gifts and prayerfully responding to the call to use those gifts and talents to share the Good News is what we are each asked to do.

Invitation to Ponder

"Since we have gifts that differ according to the grace given to us, let us exercise them: if prophecy, in proportion to the faith; if ministry, in ministering; if one is a teacher, in teaching; if one exhorts, in exhortation; if one contributes, in generosity; if one is over others, with diligence; if one does acts of mercy, with cheerfulness." (Romans 12:6–8)

Look prayerfully into your heart. What gifts have you been given that you can use to celebrate the richness of our faith throughout the liturgical year?

_____

_____

_____

_____

_____

_____

_____

_____

_____

_____

_____

_____

_____

_____

_____

_____

Connecting to Scripture

PRAYER TO THE HOLY SPIRIT BEFORE READING SCRIPTURE

Come, Holy Spirit. Fill me with every grace and blessing necessary to understand the message, prepared for and awaiting me, in the Scriptures. May I grow deeper in faith, in hope, and in love with Jesus as I spend this time with the Word of God. Amen.

🖋 Psalm 103:1–5 _____

_____

_____

🖋 2 Corinthians 5:20 _____

_____

_____

🖋 2 Corinthians 12:9–10 _____

_____

_____

🖋 Matthew 5:13–16 _____

_____

_____

🖋 Matthew 25:33–40 _____

_____

_____

Scripture Reflection

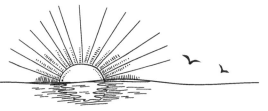

The motivation behind each celebration and tradition should be to grow in faith and in love of the Father, Son, and Holy Spirit. Of course, if they bring delight to you and your family, all the better! My suggestions for celebrations corresponding with the liturgical calendar are not meant to be a new to-do list. However, if you like to keep lists, have at it; I sure do. Once you have a few ideas, ask yourself the questions below.

Does this celebration/tradition help me to

Be genuine? Living more liturgically isn't about keeping up appearances and juggling multiple personas. Actively living the liturgical life doesn't affect us only when we're at Mass or when we're around our Christian friends. It affects and changes our very core, and hopefully becomes something people recognize within us. Instead of telling a friend that you hope things work out well when they share troubling news, tell them you'll pray for them. Instead of just saying you're busy, explain that you can't make brunch on Sunday morning because you'll be at Mass. It's a way we can each be genuine while serving as a loving witness as we go about our daily life. We are, as we read in 2 Corinthians 5:20, "ambassadors for Christ."

Be balanced? Let living more mindfully of the liturgical calendar be a part of your life, but don't be overcome by it. Incorporating every possible feast into your personal calendar is probably not the best plan of action. A new crazy list of "must-dos" would feel more like oppression than a celebration. Find ways that work for you and your home. One chicken cannot sit on every egg laid in the hen house; God does not expect you to celebrate with grandeur every saint who ever lived. Let the addition of these celebrations come naturally over time.

Be vulnerable? Starting new traditions, even in your own home, can be met with a few strange looks! A few years ago, we began to say grace before meals. It took a very (very) long time before this practice became second nature. I'll openly admit it still occasionally gives me a moment of pause when we pray before meals in restaurants or at large gatherings in our home, but I am continually surprised by the beautiful responses we receive. On numerous occasions, we have had an individual stop by our restaurant table and comment on how lovely it was to see a young family still praying before meals. Usually followed with a nostalgic comment that they used to do it as a child but somehow never continued with their own family. My son still talks about the time "that lady bought me ice cream for saying my prayers at the restaurant." (And, if you happen to be that nice lady, thank you from the bottom of my heart!) I felt scared and weak when we started being so open with our faith, yet the Lord said, "My grace is sufficient for you, for power is made perfect in weakness" (2 Corinthians 12:9). Each time we open ourselves up, feeling weak and vulnerable, grace abounds not only within us but for those around us to whom we are witnesses.

Be a witness? When you celebrate Saint Catherine of Siena's feast day with pizza (she was, after all, an Italian saint), invite your Catholic friends over to join in. Invite your non-Catholic friends too. No one turns down a free meal! "Just so, your light must shine before others, that they may see your good deeds and glorify your heavenly Father" (Matthew 5:16). Our simple everyday acts—even eating takeout—are opportunites for us to openly demonstrate our faith, chances to shine our light as we share faith and fellowship with those around us.

Be open? It's so easy to hold back from inviting a neighbor to a Friday Lenten meal, or to refrain from mealtime prayers with a coworker. Instead, be open to the Spirit's nudges. Jesus says, "For I was hungry and you gave me food, I was thirsty and you gave me drink, a stranger and you welcomed me" (Matthew 25:35). We have no way of knowing where another person is on his or her faith journey. Being open in living your faith may be a warm invitation for them to consider their beliefs. Being transparent in living your faith may provide them with an opportunity to ask honest questions about why or how you do what you do. Being open in living your faith gives you a chance to share God's love with those around you in a nonjudgmental, loving, lead-by-example way. A close friend who identified as a spiritual child of the earth a few years ago has started attending a Christian church after her daughter asked to go to church just like our son. We continually pray for this family and continue to extend invitations for them to celebrate with us. She credits their church attendance with our willingness to share our faith so openly with them. I would never have thought inviting our neighbors over so many years ago for pizza would have led to such a gift!

Be prayerful? Ask God how to share his love for you. Set time aside to listen to what he is asking of you. Imitate Mary, who pondered all in her heart. Ask him to reveal himself to you throughout the liturgical year. Whether it's attending the Stations of the Cross during Lent, saying a decade of the Rosary during the quiet hours of the morning, or making an offering of thanks as you fold laundry, create dedicated time to spend in prayer.

Be strengthened? Your faith and mine will continue to grow as God gives us grace through each and every day. It purifies us, strengthens us, and gives us chances to use our gifts and talents for a greater good. Each day we must decide to lean on God amid all the joys and hardships of life. Never forget: "I have the strength for everything through him who empowers me" (Philippians 4:13).

Contemplate the Celebration

1. What is the goal of living more mindfully of the liturgical calendar? How can living liturgically bring you closer to Christ?

_____

_____

_____

_____

_____

_____

_____

_____

2. How can you keep faith at the center of your celebrations? Is there a balance you need to achieve between secular celebrations and the way you celebrate in your home?

_____

_____

_____

_____

_____

_____

_____

_____

_____

3. Living Liturgically through Tradition: What new ways have you found to celebrate your faith throughout the year? Have you discovered other ways that you are interested in learning more about?

_____

_____

_____

_____

_____

_____

_____

_____

Closing Prayer

Renewed by my time with you, Lord, may I put into practice the inspiring teachings and traditions presented within these pages. May striving to live in relationship with you by being more liturgically minded enrich my life, my private prayer, and my sharing of the faith with others.

May I often come to you in prayer, striving to learn how to pray without ceasing, allowing my work, chores, silence, and even my leisure to be a prayer to you. May I always be in constant communion with you, and offer my gifts and talents as blessings to others. May the Word of God and the treasures of the Church live richly within me, always on my mind, in my heart, and on my lips.

During these last seven weeks, you have presented me with so many new ways to live a liturgical life, rooted in tradition and grace. May I never forget that your grace is always sufficient in whatever needs I have, that your love and mercy are always a refuge when the storms of life rage against me. May the witness of my faith glorify you. May my authentic testimony to your goodness and mercy encourage others to come to know, to love, and to serve you, my Lord and my God.

Help me, dear Lord, to be genuine, faithful, prayerful, and open to you every day of my life. Let the celebrations of my faith continue to draw me closer to you. Let the rhythm of the saints and the Church calendar fill my heart with a song of praise.

Invigorate my faith by the power of the Holy Spirit as I continue to reflect on the liturgical year, the Scriptures, and the questions to ponder. May I keep drawing closer and closer to you. Amen.

Notes

1 Congregation for Divine Worship and the Discipline of the Sacraments, *Directory on Popular Piety and the Liturgy: Principles and Guidelines* (Vatican City, December 2001), article 94.

2 Chene Heady, *Numbering My Days: How the Liturgical Calendar Rearranged My Life* (San Francisco, CA: Ignatius Press, 2016).

3 Pius Sammut, OCD, "Blessed by the Cross." FatherPius.site, accessed Sept. 30, 2019, http://www.fatherpius.site/enjoy-the-freedom-of-god/carmel/blessed-by-the-cross/.

4 Sacred Congregation for Divine Worship, *General Norms or the Liturgical Year and the Calendar*, accessed Sept. 30, 2019, https://www.catholicculture.org/culture/library/view.cfm?id=5932, article 40.

5 *General Norms for the Liturgical Year*, article 41.

6 *Directory on Popular Piety*, article 100.

7 Cindy Wooden, "Preparing for Christmas One Papal Homily at a Time," NCRonline.org, accessed Sept. 30, 2019, https://www.ncronline.org/news/vatican/preparing-christmas-one-papal-homily-time.

8 *Directory on Popular Piety*, article 108.

9 Steve Weidenkopf, "St. Boniface and the Christmas Tree," catholic.com, accessed Sept. 30, 2019, http://www.catholic.com/magazine/online-edition/st-boniface-and-the-christmas-tree.

[10] Catholic Answers, "Miracle Plays and Mysteries," catholic.com, accessed Sept. 30, 2019, https://www.catholic.com/encyclopedia /miracle-plays-and-mysteries.

[11] Paul VI, *Apostolic Constitution on Fast and Abstinence,* accessed Sept. 30, 2019, vatican.va.

[12] *Code of Canon Law*, article 1246.

[13] Keith Fournier, "Lent Begins: Ash Wednesday, Turn Away from Sin and Be Faithful to the Gospel," catholic com, accessed Sept. 30, 2019, https://www.catholic.org/lent/story.php?id=40613.

[14] *General Instruction of the Roman Missal,* article 346

[15] John Paul II, "Angelus" (November 30, 1986), accessed Sept. 30, 2019, vatican.va.

[16] Homeless World Cup Foundation, "Global Homelessness Statistics," accessed Sept. 30, 2019, https://homelessworldcup.org /homelessness-statistics/.

[17] William Saunders, "History of Lent" *Arlington Catholic Herald*, accessed Sept. 30, 2019, retrieved from https://www.catholiceducation .org/en/culture/catholic-contributions/history-of-lent.html.

[18] *Code of Cannon Law*, article 1.

[19] Saunders, William, "Disposing of Blessed Objects," *Arlington Catholic Herald*, accessed Sept. 30, 2019, retrieved from https://www .catholicculture.org/culture/library/view.cfm?recnum=3802.

[20] USCCB, "The Roman Missal and the Easter Vigil," USCCB.org, ac-

cessed Sept. 30, 2019, http://www.usccb.org/prayer-and-worship
/liturgical-year/triduum/roman-missal-and-the-easter-vigil.cfm.

[21] Maria Faustina, *Diary: Divine Mercy in My Soul* (Stockbridge, MA: Marian Press, 2011).

[22] Faustina, *Diary*.

[23] John Paul II, "Letter of Pope John Paul II to Women," accessed Sept. 30, 2019, vatican.va.

[24] USCCB, "Ordinary Time," USCCB.org, accessed Sept. 30, 2019, http://www.usccb.org/prayer-and-worship/liturgical-year/ordinary-time.cfm.

[25] Kenneth Brighenti and John Trigilio, *The Catholicism Answer Book: The 300 Most Frequently Asked Questions* (Naperville, IL: Sourcebooks, 2007).

[26] Jennifer Gregory Miller, "Contemporary Observation of Ember Days," CatholicCulture.org, accessed Sept. 30, 2019, https://www.catholicculture.org/culture/liturgicalyear/blog/index.cfm?ID=155.

[27] Joan Chittister, OSB, *The Liturgical Year: The Spiraling Adventure of the Spiritual Life* (Nashville: Thomas Nelson, 2010).

The Gift of Invitation:
7 Ways That Jesus Invites You to a Life of Grace
(Stay Connected Journals for Catholic Women)

By Allison Gingras

You're invited to something wonderful — a more abundant life and a closer relationship with God — all you need to do is respond.

In **The Gift of Invitation: 7 Ways Jesus Invites You to a Life of Grace**, you will:

- Discover the seven powerful invitations Jesus extends to you, including the invitation to follow him, forgive from your heart, and know his Father's many gifts

- Explore the Bible to develop a deeper relationship with Jesus

- See how each invitation plays out in your own life

- Reflect on how you can be better prepared to accept Jesus' invitations.

Perfect for individual or group study, the seven chapters includes reflections and scripture, with space for journaling.

Becoming Holy, One Virtue at a Time:
A Guide to Living the Theological and Cardinal Virtues
(Stay Connected Journals for Catholic Women)

By Sara Estabrooks

God calls each of us to become saints. That may seem daunting, but in **Becoming Holy, One Virtue at a Time**, Sara Estabrooks shows you how you can answer this call in your daily life. By drawing on Scripture and the Catechism of the Catholic Church, you will be enabled to seek virtue and pursue sainthood, starting now.

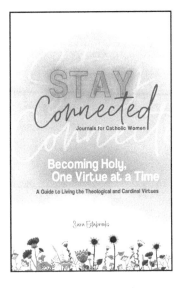

In **Becoming Holy, One Virtue at a Time** you will:

• Grow in understanding of the theological and cardinal virtues;

• Dive into biblical stories that inspire you to become the person God made you to be;

• Reflect on your vocation to holiness in your daily life; and

• Accept God's call to live a life of virtue.